Diane Phalen *quilts*

10 Projects to Celebrate the Seasons

Diane Beginnes-Phalen

C&T PUBLISHING

Copyright ©2000 by Diane Beginnes-Phalen
Graphic Illustrations ©2000 by C&T Publishing

Developmental Editor: Cyndy Lyle Rymer
Technical Editor: Joyce Engels Lytle
Copyeditor: Steve Cook
Project Editors: Joyce Engels Lytle, Lynn Koolish, and Sara MacFarland
Book Design: Staci Harpole, Cubic Design
Cover Design and Graphic Illustrations: Aliza Kahn
Production Direction: Kathy Lee and Diane Pedersen
Production Assistant: Kirstie L. McCormick
Front Cover Quilt: Maple Leaf quilt made by Tiffany Burrow from fabrics graciously donated by Benartex Inc. Thread provided by Coats and Clark. Photograph by Sharon Risedorph.
Interior Photos: Photography of quilts by Sharon Risedorph; photography of paintings by Wy´ East Color Inc., Portland Oregon; photos on pages 5, 14, 42 (upper right) by Joel Tressler; all other photos by Diane Beginnes-Phalen.
Many thanks to Sherry and Bob Tankard for lending us their front porch for the cover photo.

Attention Teachers:
C&T Publishing, Inc. encourages you to use this book as a text for teaching. Contact us at 800-284-1114 or www.ctpub.com for more information about the C&T Teachers Program.

Library of Congress Cataloging-in-Publication Data

Beginnes-Phalen, Diane
    Diane Phalen quilts : ten projects to celebrate the seasons / Diane Beginnes-Phalen.
        p. cm.
Includes bibliographical references and index.
    ISBN 1-57120-106-8 (paper trade)
    1. Quilting—Patterns. 2. Patchwork—Patterns. 3. Beginnes-Phalen, Diane 4. Watercolorists—United States. I. Title.
    TT835 .B332 2000
    746.46'041—dc21
                                                    00-008285

Published by C&T Publishing, Inc.
P.O. Box 1456
Lafayette, California 94549

Printed in China
10   9   8   7   6   5   4   3   2   1

To everyone at C&T Publishing–Todd Hensley, Trish Katz, Cyndy Rymer, Liz Aneloski, Joyce Lytle, Kathy Lee, and Staci Harpole–thank you for the enthusiasm and hard work you put into making this book a reality.

Special thanks to all the talented quilters–Barbara Baker, Tiffany Burrow, Michelle Crawford, Joyce Lytle, and Nancy Odom–who gave so graciously of their time and skills in making the quilts. Thank you for sharing your wonderful talents in bringing my paintings to life! Thanks to Joel Tressler of *Stitchworld*, Norcross, Georgia for the wonderful photos.

Thanks also to the manufacturers who graciously donated the fabric and threads for the projects: Benartex Inc., Coats and Clark, Northcott/ Monarch Fabrics, P&B Textiles, Richard Kaufman Fine Fabrics, and RJR Fashion Fabrics.

Finally, a very special thank you to all of the collectors of my art–because of your enthusiasm and appreciation I will always be inspired to paint the next watercolor.

To the wonderful people in my life who always encouraged my artistic endeavors: my husband, Mike; my parents, John and Arlene Beginnes; my sisters Linda, Mary, and Anne; my in-laws, John and Mary Lou Phalen; and my office manager, Michelle Sexton.

To all the quilters throughout the world for sharing your love and joy of quilting with me. Your enthusiasm for my watercolors and wonderful friendship has been a real bright spot in my life! As many of you know, I have never made a quilt...at least not with a machine or needle or thread! My love is to make watercolor quilts with paints and brushes. Without your beautiful creations I would have no inspiration. I am spellbound by your talents and generous spirit.

With all the support and love surrounding me I am truly blessed!

Happy Quilting to all! I hope to see you and your finished projects at the next quilt show!

CONTENTS

Page 31

Page 46

Page 51

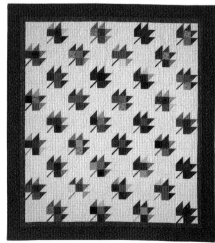

Page 49

Page 34

Page 59

CONTENTS

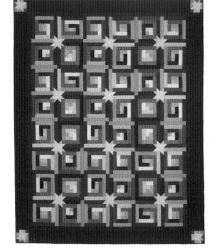

Page 63

Page 95

Page 72

Page 78

Page 89

INTRODUCTION

I live in rural Oregon in a secluded house nestled on seventeen wooded acres. A creek meanders through the property. My husband Mike and I live with our family pets—a golden retriever named Bogie, two cats named Socks and Gato, and a cockatiel named Oz. The woods surrounding us is home to deer, raccoons, coyotes, squirrels, and many of our fine feathered friends, such as chickadees, woodpeckers, juncos, and finches.

◀ *Mt. Hood and Chickadees*

INTRODUCTION

I have lived most of my life in the rural countryside. I was born and raised in Bethlehem, Pennsylvania, where my mom, dad, and three sisters still live. As a Pennsylvania native, I grew up in the midst of gentle rolling hills and farmland. The countryside included such wonderful features as old barns, churches, covered bridges, mills, country stores, one-room schoolhouses, and historic buildings. Nearby was an Amish community, which fascinated me and constantly drew me to explore the backroads and enjoy the solitude. It was this solitude that helped me discover my love of sketching. I spent hours drawing and observing nature. Many years later, when I moved to the West Coast, it would be these memories and feelings I would paint. Today a certain smell or a nostalgic mood will bring these images and feelings flooding back. I find that emotions and memories are a large part of my creative process.

Scenes from Bethlehem, Pennsylvania and the surrounding countryside.

◀ *Summer Afternoon Geese*

When I decided on the subject matter of my art, I was naturally inclined to combine the rural landscape of my youth with the lovely quilts I so frequently saw hanging from porch rails, clotheslines, and fences. My initial inspiration to include quilts in my paintings came after one of my many visits to see my family in Pennsylvania. I had been living on the West Coast for six years, painting wildlife and landscapes. I was traveling on one of my many backroad trips gathering inspiration for painting ideas when I came across an old country store in the town of Stony Run, Pennsylvania. I spent several hours photographing and sketching Hosfelds' General Store. In a nearby shop I saw some lovely quilts hanging and, with the owner's permission, took photographs.

My fascination with quilts increased after I completed my first watercolor entitled *Country Store Quilts*. The *Americana Quilt Series* was born

Special places that inspired my first paintings.

and has been going strong for the past ten years. I find it difficult to *not* include a quilt in my paintings and like to say, "I quilt with my paintbrush!" I know most of the traditional patterns and even the basics of quiltmaking. Some day I hope to try my hand at quilting. As of this writing I have finished forty paintings in the *Americana Quilt Series* with a total of over ninety quilts between them. Log Cabin, Double Wedding Ring, Lone Star, Bears' Paw—the quilt designs are endless, and I want to paint them all!

The wonderful thing about that first quilt painting was that it introduced me to the special world of quilting. I began to set up a booth at quilt shows and met the most congenial group of people. I do many local quilt shows and travel to some favorite shows, such as the annual International Quilt Market and Festival in Houston, Texas; Quilter's Heritage in Lancaster, Pennsylvania; and the Sisters Outdoor Quilt Show™ in Sisters, Oregon. I especially enjoy meeting and talking with the many quilters. I find their quilts so emotional and inspiring. The same elements that are in painting are present in quilting: considerations of effect, color scheme, design style, and color balance.

My studio is located over the detached garage behind our house, and is surrounded by trees and nature. It is a wonderful place to paint. I have three large drawing tables that I use to design,

sketch, and paint—I paint 8 to 10 hours per day. I love to get "lost" in my paintings and travel back to the place where the inspiration and emotion for the idea first appeared. I also love to paint with the seasons. I gather my emotional response to the arrival of spring, summer, autumn, and winter. The quilts featured in each painting are a large part of my response.

With the arrival of spring, crocuses push up through the snow and quilts are hung on clotheslines for airing and to absorb the fresh spring air. Summer brings the warm caress of a summer breeze that gently flaps quilts on the line to dry. Autumn is rich in color, and harvest-colored quilts are hung outside a general store, with the crisp coolness and earthy scent of apples, leaves, and pumpkins mingling in the air. Quilts are also present on a snowy winter's eve with holiday quilts airing in expectation of arriving friends and family who will be warm and cozy beneath their downy weight.

I will continue to travel the rural backroads for inspiration and to soak up emotions and memories to paint. I make annual visits to Lancaster County, home to many Amish, and through the years I have become even more enamored with the beautiful countryside and the simple lifestyle of the Amish. I love listening to the silence of the countryside.

I am amazed at how the Amish manage to stay focused on their farming, crafts, and quiltmaking. It greatly saddens me to see civilization interfere with their peaceful ways. It breaks my heart to see a beautiful Amish farm surrounded by modern homes and the electrical wires that have come with this urbanization. I hope through my paintings to share the beauty of the remaining countryside and to help preserve the beautiful barns, covered bridges, mill ponds, and country stores that are a part of so many of our memories and history.

The *Americana Quilt Series* will always be an ongoing love affair of my heart. The quilts are such a part of my emotion and heritage; they curl around me with their warmth in the images of my memories of Pennsylvania, family, and home.

▲ *Quiet Afternoon*

S P R I N G

pring awakens the world with beautiful
pastels in pink, purple, yellow, and red. The ground
comes alive with the warmth of the sun reaching
beneath the snow. I always find it fascinating that the
flower bulbs and seeds know when to awaken. The
first crocus and snowdrops come up through the snow,
somehow knowing that the snow doesn't matter;
spring is on its way!

◀ *Spring Dance*

In *Spring Dance* (page 16), the garden seeds have arrived from the mail-order catalogs. It is time to plant and dig in the moist, earthy soil that has finally thawed from the winter chill of ice and snow. We can bid farewell to the drab browns and grays of winter. The soil around the house and in the surrounding fields and meadows will soon be filled with bright, colorful flowers.

The sun touches the hanging quilts with its warm rays, making them smell sweet and fresh.

Flowering trees are in full bloom. Soon they will lose their petals, which will drift and fall to the ground like autumn leaves. Budding leaves make their first appearance, a bright and shiny yellow-green that later matures into the warm dark greens of summer.

Signs of spring in the Amish countryside.

Daffodils by Porch ▶

DIANE PHALEN ©

A Beautiful Spring Day in Lancaster County, Pennsylvania

Every spring I return to my native state of Pennsylvania to visit family and friends. I plan my yearly visit so it coincides with the Quilter's Heritage Quilt Show held in Lancaster. I always have a great time at the show, visiting with friends I have not seen all year. The day after the show is spent driving the wonderful winding backroads of Lancaster County. Beautiful Amish farms, homes, and one-room schoolhouses dot the countryside. When I am here feelings of happiness and peace pass over me. I have stepped back to a time in which the pace is slower and you can hear the quiet. Families gather to talk, to worship, to farm, and to enjoy life the way it was meant to be enjoyed. The Amish are in tune with the earth and Mother Nature. In the spring and summer months planting, gardening, and field work takes top priority. Spring planting is done without a tractor–or its noise.

As I continue my journey I am very excited to see a red dot on the horizon–a covered bridge! I spend a long time sitting by the creek that runs below the bridge. As I walk through the covered bridge, I enjoy smelling the old wood and watching the water through the openings in the wooden floor.

Generations of Amish sometimes live and work on the same homestead. I come across a group of three houses together. Everyone works together, farming, quilting, and keeping the home.

I love the sight of an Amish clothesline swaying in the breeze. Amish women and children wear plain but colorful dresses underneath a black smock or apron. The men wear shirts made in colors that range from blues and greens to browns, purples, and crimson. The women of the family do all the sewing, which leaves them with a wide assortment of fabric remnants to be used in their quilts. A true Amish quilt is one of my favorite things!

I continue along the backroads, often stopping to take photographs and enjoy the beauty of my surroundings. I pass by many one-room schoolhouses where children are outside playing. It is lunchtime, and the children play a game of tag and baseball. Other children sit in groups giggling and telling stories. I enjoy listening to their laughter but do not take any photographs, as I feel it would be intrusive.

Spring plowing is being done in every field. I continue to drive by stone mills, ponds, Amish horse and buggies, farm animals, and many roadside stands. I stop for lunch at one Amish stand. They are selling my favorite baked goody: shoo-fly pie! The Amish farmers have expanded their interests to include many cottage industries. They sell baked goods as well as vegetables and fruits at the roadside stands. You can also find beautiful quilts for sale, along with hand-made

furniture, toys, and decorative garden accessories. The Amish do not have telephones in their homes, but for their small businesses they allow outhouse-style telephone booths in their fields!

I see several signs along my way that say "Quilts for Sale." I pass many lovely Amish homes with quilts hanging on the front porch. They are so beautiful that I stop to admire and photograph them. Inside the home, many beautiful quilts cover several beds. Quilted potholders, Amish dolls, wallhangings–all handmade–are also for sale. Through a window I see a small Amish boy and girl playing underneath a clothesline. They take turns pulling each other in a red wagon.

Today is special for me because I have been invited to visit a friend. Susie Riehl is an Amish artist, a mother of six, as well as a quilter! Her paintings, like mine, also include quilts. Susie welcomes me

Scenes from Lancaster County Amish country.

into her warm, wonderfully sunny kitchen, where she has graciously prepared some baked goods and mint tea. The kitchen is the heart of the home and where the family gathers; the kitchen table does double-duty as Susie's studio. Another friend, Shirley Wengert, joins us. Shirley owns Double Heart Gallery in Ronks, Pennsylvania, and is Susie's agent and representative. We pass the afternoon chatting and enjoying our tea and wonderful sweet desserts. A tour of the farm includes a brief visit to her husband John's workshop and woodworking business. Then it's time to say goodbye and thanks for a wonderful day.

As I drive around the backroads by Susie's home, I pass several Amish children on rollerblades, skating home at the end of their school day. My last stop before I must leave this magical place is Jacob Zook's Hex Signs. Because of my

Pennsylvania Dutch heritage, I have always enjoyed these colorful signs and displayed them in my home. Doves, lilies, hearts and tulips, stars, geometric patterns, and teardrops make up many of the patterns for the hex signs. Hex signs are mainly used as barn decorations, and are of German origin. They can also be found on hope chests and in some decorations, as well as on family bibles, where they are used as decorative borders. The Amish do not display the signs on their barns, as they are considered "fancy." The same hex designs are found in quilts, such as LeMoyne Star, Pinwheel, and Churn Dash to name only a few. I find several Hex signs to add to my collection. As I return to my car, the sun is beginning to set, and I say a last farewell to my beautiful surroundings. I look forward to coming "home" again in the spring next year.

Susie Riehl's Farm

Baskets and Bunnies ▶

A Visit to Schreiner's Iris Farm, Oregon

I had a wonderful time in Pennsylvania enjoying early spring. Upon my return to Oregon in early May, I get to experience spring again! This year, due to very wet and cold weather, flowers and blossoms are late in arriving on the West Coast. The fields are planted in crimson red clover. The countryside abounds with lilacs, irises, and rhododendrons.

My favorite Oregon spring excursion is an annual visit to Schreiner's Iris Gardens in Keizer. On a beautiful day in May, I awaken to a blue, sunny sky. Oregon does not experience many days as picture-perfect as this, so I decide to abandon my studio and spend a day among the irises.

I travel down the backroads in a southerly direction. In a little over an hour the first signs appear, directing me to the iris fields. All of a

Scenes from Schreiner's Iris Gardens.

sudden, acres and acres of planted irises appear, row after row of color. It is a breathtaking sight!

I park my car and follow my nose to the viewing gardens. The fragrance is heavenly. I begin taking photographs, stopping to read the names and description of each iris.

They have names like "Midnight Dancer," "Last Hurrah," "Trails West," and "Stitch in Time." I finally put my camera away–the irises need to be enjoyed with all my senses, not just through the camera lens. I bring out my sketch pad and draw their ruffled, lacy shapes. I spend several hours walking, enjoying the irises and this perfect spring day.

It's time to head back home. As I approach my car I see a sign that says "irises for sale," and I buy a dozen of the beautiful irises. I return to share my day and the wonderful fragrance with my husband, Mike.

Spring Heart Wreath Quilt

Machine appliquéd and quilted by Nancy Odom.

"Almost solid" and tone-on-tone fabrics were chosen for this quilt for their multicolor, painterly quality in a loose interpretation of the color scheme of Diane's quilt. The beautiful pastels suggested by spring flowers bloom in this heartful appliqué quilt that would make a wonderful gift or family heirloom.

◄ Spring Patchwork

Fabrics for the quilt shown were graciously donated by Northcott Silk Inc. from their Black, White and Ivory Basics; Clouds; and Basics by Diana Leone collections. Thread was donated by Coats and Clark.

Finished Size: 84 1/2" x 104 1/2"

Blocks Set: 3 x 4

Block Size: 20" finished, 6 with wreath and heart appliqués, 6 with heart appliqués

FABRIC REQUIREMENTS

White Background: 3 3/4 yards (if fabric is more than 43" wide), 7 1/4 yards if fabric is less than 43" wide

Hearts: 2/3 yard each of light violet and pink

Leaves: 1/8 yard each of dark violet, purple, turquoise, dark green, and yellow fabrics

Wreath Vine: 1 yard for 1/4"-wide finished bias strips. Leftover fabric can be used for leaves.

Inner Border: 1 yard (same green as Wreath)

Outer Border: 2 1/2 yards (leftovers can be used for leaves)

Backing: 7 1/2 yards

Batting: 88" x 108"

Binding: 2/3 yard

Bias bar: 1/4"-wide bar for vine

Template plastic or fusible paper-backed adhesive

CUTTING

The template patterns for the hearts and leaves are on page 105.

Background Squares: Cut twelve 21 1/2" squares

Hearts: Cut 48 light violet and 48 pink hearts

Leaves: Cut 132 leaves total. Be sure to cut some of the leaves with the template reversed.

Wreath Vine: Cut six 7/8" x 44" bias strips.

BORDERS

Before you cut the borders, follow the instructions in the General Guidelines (page 102), and check the final measurements of your quilt top. Adjust the border cutting lengths if necessary.

Inner Border: Cut eight 3 1/2"-wide strips. Sew together into one long strip. Cut two 80 1/2" lengths for sides and two 66 1/2" lengths for top and bottom.

Outer Border: Cut nine 9 1/2"-wide strips. Sew together into one long strip. Cut two 86 1/2" lengths for sides and two 84 1/2" lengths for top and bottom.

BLOCK ASSEMBLY

Use the appliqué technique of your choice to complete the blocks. The quilter chose to fuse the appliqué shapes onto the background squares, and machine stitch the edges using a blanket stitch. You can choose a more traditional hand appliqué needle-turn or freezer paper method; or machine stitch the appliqué pieces using a zigzag or satin stitch.

In preparation for appliqué, press each 21 1/2" background square in half diagonally, vertically, and horizontally to find the center of the block and to create guideline folds.

HEART BLOCKS

Arrange four of the hearts in the center of the block, placing the vertical center of each heart on one of the fold lines with the bottom point of the finished heart about 1/8" from the center. The other four hearts should be placed on the diagonal in each of the four corners, approximately 7/8" from the outside edge of the fabric. Baste, glue, or fuse all hearts in place. Machine or hand appliqué. Use photo for reference.

WREATH BLOCKS

1. Begin by creating the center vine for the wreath. Cut bias

strips $^7/_8$" wide and piece diagonally as necessary for a total of six 44"-long pieces. With wrong sides together, fold the bias strip in half lengthwise, and stitch about $^1/_8$" from the outside edge. Insert the bias bar, and press on both sides with the seam centered on the back side.

2. The outside edge of the vine is a 13" diameter circle around the center of the block. Place the bias strip on the right side of the background fabric with the seam allowance facing down. Baste or lightly glue the vine in place, then appliqué using desired method.

3. Arrange the four hearts in the center of each block and the leaves on each side of the vine. Use the diagram and photo for reference. Baste, fuse, or lightly glue in place. Appliqué the hearts and leaves using desired method.

QUILT TOP ASSEMBLY

1. Trim all blocks to 20$^1/_2$".

2. Arrange the blocks as shown.

3. Sew the blocks together in horizontal rows. Press the seams of alternate rows in opposite directions. Sew the

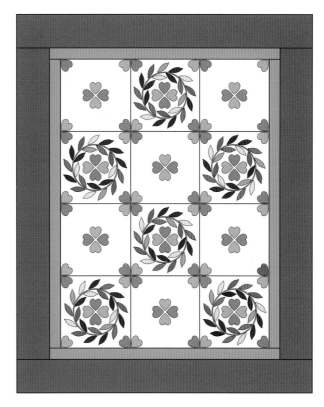

Quilt Assembly

horizontal rows together. Gently press the quilt top.

4. Add the inner side borders first, press seam toward the border. Add the inner top and bottom borders, press toward the border.

5. Repeat Step 4 for the outer border.

QUILTING

This would be a perfect quilt to exercise your imagination on the quilting pattern; flowers, hearts, or grid quilting could be used to highlight the lovely appliqué. If your quilt is to become a family heirloom, hand quilting would enhance its

sentimental value; but machine quilting (as in our pictured quilt) is equally effective.

Our quilter stitched "in-the-ditch" around the outside edges of the leaves, wreaths, and the hearts. On the blocks without appliquéd wreaths, she used a wreath pattern for her quilting design. The rest of the background was quilted in a random meandering pattern. For the first border she used a small wandering leaf pattern. On the outer border a larger-scale version of the wandering leaf has been combined with swirls in a random meandering style.

Tulips in a Vase Quilt

Machine pieced and quilted by Barbara Baker.

This charming wallhanging was made using spring pastels with a dazzling blue for accent.
Our quilter used small prints that read as "almost solids," but it would be an ideal quilt to use the
currently popular hand-dyed fabrics. It would also be striking done in stronger, basic colors.
Use your imagination or refer to gardening catalogs and books for more color ideas.

Fabrics for the quilt and pillow shown were graciously donated by R.J.R. Fashion Fabrics from their Bare Essentials and Basic Realities collections. Thread was donated by Coats and Clark.

Finished Quilt Size: 34 1/2" square

Blocks Set: 2 x 2

Block Size: 12" finished

FABRIC REQUIREMENTS

White Background: 3/4 yard

Pink for Tulips, Sashing, and Inner Border: 5/8 yard

Green: 3/8 yard

Yellow: 1/8 yard

Blue for Vases, Outer Border, and Binding: 1 yard

Backing: 1 yard

Batting: 38" square

Template Plastic

CUTTING

The template pattern for the stem is on page 106.

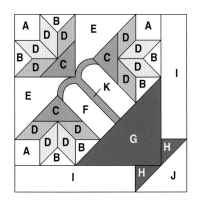

Tulips in a Vase

White:

* Cut one 2 1/4"-wide strip into twelve 2 1/4" squares (A).
* Cut six 3 3/4" squares, then cut diagonally twice into 24 quarter-square triangles (B).
* Cut four 5 1/8" squares, then cut diagonally into 8 half-square triangles (E).
* Cut four 4" x 4 3/4" rectangles (F).
* Cut two 2 1/4"-wide strips into eight 2 1/4" x 9" rectangles (I).
* Cut two 4 3/8" squares, then cut diagonally into 4 half-square triangles (J).

Pink:

Cut two 1 3/4"-wide strips. Then position the 45° line of the ruler on the edge of the fabric and cut one end of the strip. Keeping the 45° line on the fabric's edge, slide the ruler over 1 3/4" and cut. Repeat until you have 24 diamonds (D) for the quilt. Or make a template from the D diamond pattern provided on page 106.

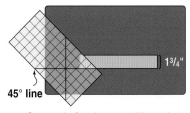

Cut end of strip at a 45° angle.

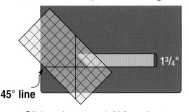

Slide ruler over 1 3/4" and cut.

Sashing Strips:

Cut two 2 1/2"-wide strips, then cut the strips into two 12 1/2" lengths and one 26 1/2" length.

Green:

* Cut three 3 3/4" squares, then cut them diagonally twice into 12 quarter-square triangles (C).
* Make a template for the stem pattern on page 106, and cut four stems (K).

Yellow:

Cut two 1 3/4"-wide strips. Then position the 45° line of the ruler on the edge of the fabric and cut one end of the strip. With the 45° line still on the edge of the fabric, slide the ruler over 1 3/4" and cut. Repeat until you have 24 diamonds (D).

Blue:

* Cut two 6 7/8" squares, then cut diagonally into 4 half-square triangles (G).
* Cut four 2 5/8" squares, then cut diagonally into 8 half-square triangles (H).

BORDERS

Before you cut the borders, follow the instructions in the General Guidelines (page 102), and check the final measurements of your quilt top.

Adjust the border cutting lengths if necessary.

Pink Inner Border:

❋ Cut two 2½" x 26½" strips for the top and bottom borders.

❋ Cut two 2½" x 30½" strips for the side borders.

Blue Outer Border:

❋ Cut two 2½" x 30½" strips for the top and bottom borders.

❋ Cut two 2½" x 34½" strips for the side borders.

BLOCK ASSEMBLY

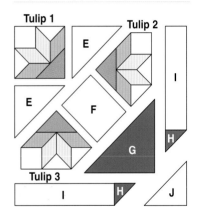

Make four blocks for the quilt top, one block for the pillow.

Note: Since the white square A is placed differently in each flower, it is helpful to lay out all the pieces for each block before sewing together.

1. Mark a dot ¼" in from the corner of the white B triangles and white A squares on the wrong side of the fabric. This is the start and stop point for the Y seam.

2. For Tulip 1, sew a pink D and a yellow D to a white B. Sew in the direction of the arrows, backstitching at the dot. Make two D/B/D units. Press as indicated.
For Tulips 2 and 3 make one D/B/D unit. Follow layout of block.

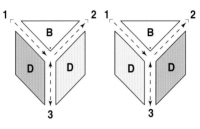

Seam 3 can be sewn in either direction.

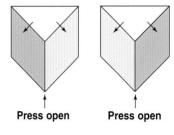

Press open   Press open

3. For Tulip 1, sew an A square to a D/B/D unit. Backstitch at the dot. Press as indicated.

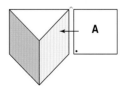

Then sew the A/D/B/D unit to the other D/B/D unit as shown.

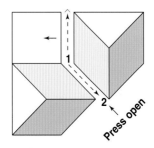

Backstitch at the dot. Press as indicated.

Attach green triangle C as shown. Press as indicated.

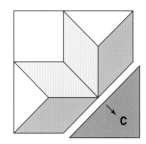

4. For Tulips 2 and 3, sew a pink and a yellow D to an A square. Backstitch at the dot. Press as indicated.

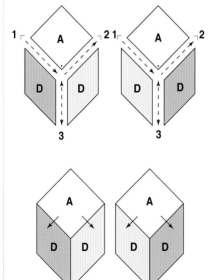

Press open   Press open

5. Sew a pink/yellow D/A/D unit to a white B triangle and a yellow/pink D/B/D unit. Backstitch at the dot. Press as indicated.

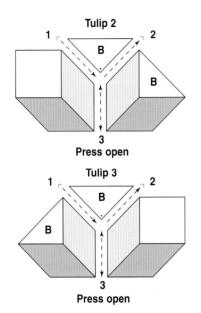

Tulip 2

B

B

Press open

Tulip 3

B

B

Press open

Attach green triangle C as shown in Step 3. Press seam toward the C triangle.

6. Sew a white E triangle to each side of Tulip 1. Press seam toward the E triangles.

7. Sew Tulip 2 to white F rectangle to Tulip 3. Press seams toward the F rectangle.

Then sew E/Tulip 1/E unit to Tulip 2/F/Tulip 3 unit. Press seam toward the E/Tulip 1/E unit.

8. Appliqué green stem K.

9. Attach blue triangle G (seam will cover raw end of stem appliqué). Press toward triangle G.

10. Sew a blue H triangle to the end of each white I strip. Press toward H triangle.

11. Attach H/I strips to the sides of the Tulips/E/F/G unit. Press seam toward H/I strips.

12. Attach white triangle J. Press seam toward J triangle.

QUILT ASSEMBLY

1. Referring to the diagram, sew a pink $2^{1}/_{2}$" x $12^{1}/_{2}$" sashing strip between two tulip blocks. Press seams toward the sashing. Repeat with the remaining two blocks.

2. Sew these two vertical "rows" to each side of a pink $2^{1}/_{2}$" x $26^{1}/_{2}$" strip. Press seam toward the sashing.

3. Add the inner top and bottom border lengths, press toward the border. Add the inner side borders, press toward the border. Repeat for the outer border.

QUILTING

Our quilter machine stitched a slight curve inside the tulip petals from petal point to point, leaving the green stem appliqués and flower bases unquilted. She used a modified grid pattern on the blue "vase" and a random meandering stitch in the back-ground and into the sashing and inner border. She stitched a single broad swag pattern in the outer border.

Quilt Assembly

Tulips in a Vase Pillow, 18" square, machine pieced by Barbara Baker.

FABRIC REQUIREMENTS

White: ¹/₄ yard
Pink: ¹/₄ yard
Yellow: ¹/₈ yard
Blue: ³/₈ yard
Green: ¹/₂ yard
18" Pillow form
Template plastic

CUTTING

The template pattern for the stem is on page 106.

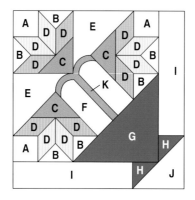

Tulips in a Vase

White:

❋ Cut three 2¹/₄" squares (A).
❋ Cut two 3³/₄" squares, then cut diagonally twice into 8 quarter-square triangles (B). Need only 6.

❋ Cut one 5¹/₈" square, then cut diagonally into 2 half-square triangles (E).
❋ Cut one 4" x 4³/₄" rectangle (F).
❋ Cut two 2¹/₄" x 9" rectangles (I).
❋ Cut one 4³/₈" square, then cut diagonally into 2 half-square triangles (J). Need only 1.

Pink:

❋ Cut two 1¹/₂"-wide strips, then cut the strips into two 12¹/₂" lengths and two 14¹/₂" lengths.
❋ Cut one 1³/₄"-wide strip. Follow instructions for cutting pink diamonds on page 35. Cut 6 diamonds (D).

Green:

❋ Cut one 3³/₄" square, then cut it diagonally twice into 4 quarter-square triangles (C).
❋ Cut one stem (K) using stem pattern on page 107.

Pillow back: Cut two 14" x 18¹/₂" rectangles.

Yellow:

Cut one 1³/₄"-wide strip. Follow instructions for cutting yellow diamonds on page 35. Cut 6 diamonds (D).

Blue:

❀ Cut two $2^1/_2$"-wide strips, then cut each strip into a $14^1/_2$" length and $18^1/_2$" length for the outer border.

❀ Cut one $6^7/_8$" square, then cut diagonally into 2 half-square triangles (G). Need only 1.

❀ Cut one $2^5/_8$" square, then cut diagonally into 2 half-square triangles (H).

PILLOW ASSEMBLY

1. Make one block according to the block assembly instructions on page 36.

2. Following the diagram above, add the $1^1/_2$" x $12^1/_2$" pink strips to each side of the block. Add two $1^1/_2$" x $14^1/_2$" pink strips to the remaining two sides of the block. Press seams toward the border.

3. Add the $2^1/_2$" x $14^1/_2$" blue strips to the sides of the block, then add the $2^1/_2$" x $18^1/_2$" blue strips to the remaining sides. Press seams toward the border.

4. **Backing:** Two overlapping pieces are used for the pillow backing (green was used for our pillow). To form finished edges on each backing piece, press under $1/_4$" along one $18^1/_2$" edge. Then press under an additional $1/_4$" and topstitch.

5. Overlap the two pieces, topstitched edges toward the center, to create an $18^1/_2$" square. Pin at the center to temporarily hold the two sides together.

6. Pin and sew the backing with right sides together to the pillow top, using a $1/_4$" seam allowance.

7. Trim the corners, and turn right side out. Press.

8. Insert the pillow form.

DIANE PHALEN©

S U M M E R

While I was growing up in Pennsylvania, summer days were spent with my three sisters riding bicycles, swimming at the local pool, and doing craft projects. As we got older we started moving in different directions, but childhood memories of those lazy summer days (and family vacations with Mom and Dad) will stay with us always. You probably have your own special summer memories. Maybe they include thoughts of gentle, peaceful breezes, and daydreaming and reading next to a bubbling creek in the shade of a willow tree. Perhaps your memory is of a huge front porch and swing, where you sipped iced tea and lemonade.

◀ *Summer Dream*

Outdoor Quilt Show in Sisters, Oregon

In the painting *Summer Dream* (page 40), the log cabin sits next to a cool mountain stream with a willow chair and my two cats, Socks and Gato. As is usual for these two, Gato is asleep and Socks is thinking of waking her and taking over that comfortable spot for himself. The mountains seen in the background are part of the view in Sisters, Oregon. I would be remiss not to mention this beautiful area of the Cascades, located in central Oregon. Sisters is not only noted for its beautiful mountains and scenery but also is home to the largest outdoor quilt festival. It takes place the second Saturday of July, and the entire town participates. The town is transformed into a backdrop for hundreds of quilts. Quilts hang from balconies, storefronts, and fence rails. Unknowing motorists gape in astonishment as they inch through town, staring at the thousands of quilters

Scenes from the Sisters Outdoor Quilt Show™.

who fill the streets and at the incredible quilts that flap in the breeze. The sense of quilter camaraderie is wonderful!

On this very special day I sign my artwork at the Folk Arts & Company gallery, which represents my artwork year round. I chat with people from as far away as England, Japan, and Australia who have come

especially to see this show. It is a wonderful celebration of quilts and the art of quilt making. It's often a hot day, but the time passes quickly as I make so many new friends.

There is another place close by which is special to me: the Patterson Ranch, one of the largest llama ranches in Oregon. I spend several hours watching the llamas graze and play in the acres of meadows surrounding the ranch. They are very gentle and curious animals; if you're lucky, they'll come right up to the fence to say hello. But don't get too close–if frightened they tend to spit!

A Day at Cannon Beach

I have included a beach scene, simply titled *Summer at the Beach*. It is a warm, sunny day.

Can't you can smell the salty air and hear the seagulls and ocean waves? The summer breeze is perfect for kite flying as well as sailing.

The West Coast beaches and shoreline are very different from the East Coast beaches I knew when I was growing up. We were only three hours from the New Jersey shore, and because Mike's parents live in Ocean City, New Jersey, I'm still fortunate enough to visit. I love walking the beach and the surrounding boardwalk when we go.

When I moved to the West Coast twenty years ago, it was incredible to drive along the coastline. The beaches were expansive and secluded, unlike the crowded beaches I knew in the East. After settling in Santa Maria, California, I spent every moment I could touring Santa Barbara, Carmel, Pismo Beach, and Avila Beach. I divided my time, first sketching and painting, then just watching the waves roll in and listening to the solitude.

My travels took me further up the coast to the Santa Cruz mountains, and eventually north to the beautiful Oregon coastline. I love the beaches here, even though they're often covered in mist and rain. I love the rock formations, and I spend a lot of time walking and sketching. My favorite beach is Cannon Beach in northern Oregon. The town of Cannon Beach is full of quaint shops and courtyards with beautiful flowers and fountains.

▼ *Summer at the Beach*

Streak of Lightning Quilt

Machine pieced and quilted by Michele Y. Crawford.

To make the patriotic quilt shown in Diane's painting (page 40), red and white tone-on-tone
fabrics were chosen for the stripes, with the red used again as the second border.
The blue triangles and third border are a medium blue, and the first and fourth outside borders are a darker blue.
This quilt pattern typically is made with traditional Amish solid colors.

Fabrics for the quilt and pillows shown were graciously donated by Northcott Silk/Monarch from their Black, White, and Ivory Basics (White), "Quilt for a Cure" Basics (Darker and Medium Blue), and Shalimar Basics (Lighter Red). Thread was donated by Coats and Clark.

Finished Quilt Size:
$62\frac{1}{2}$" X $90\frac{1}{2}$" (Twin bed size)
Blocks Set: 6 x 10
Block Size: 7" finished

FABRIC REQUIREMENTS
Red: $1\frac{5}{8}$ yards (includes Border 2)
White: $1\frac{1}{4}$ yards
Medium Blue for Background Triangles and Border 3: $2\frac{1}{4}$ yards
Dark blue (or navy) for Borders 1 and 4: $1\frac{5}{8}$ yards
Backing: 5 yards
Batting: 66" x 94"
Binding: $\frac{5}{8}$ yard

CUTTING
STRIPS
Cut twenty-five $1\frac{1}{2}$"-wide strips from both the red and white fabrics.

Medium Blue Triangles:
Cut six $7\frac{7}{8}$"-wide strips into thirty $7\frac{7}{8}$" squares. Cut the squares in half diagonally to make 60 triangles.

BORDERS
Before you cut the borders, follow the instructions in the General Guidelines (page 102), and check the final measurements of your quilt top. Adjust the border cutting lengths if necessary.

Border 1 (Dark Blue):
Cut six 3"-wide strips. Join the strips together end to end with diagonal seams into one long strip. Cut two $42\frac{1}{2}$" lengths for the top and bottom borders. Cut two $75\frac{1}{2}$" lengths for the side borders.

Border 2 (Red):
Cut seven $1\frac{1}{2}$"-wide strips. Join strips together end to end with diagonal seams into one long strip. Cut two $47\frac{1}{2}$" lengths for the top and bottom borders. Cut two $77\frac{1}{2}$" lengths for the side borders.

Border 3 (Medium Blue):
Cut seven 3"-wide strips. Join strips together end to end with diagonal seams into one long strip. Cut two $49\frac{1}{2}$" lengths for the top and bottom borders. Cut two $82\frac{1}{2}$" lengths for the side borders.

Border 4 (Dark Blue):
Cut eight $4\frac{1}{2}$"-wide strips. Join strips together end to end with diagonal seams into one long strip. Cut two $54\frac{1}{2}$" lengths for top and bottom borders. Cut two $90\frac{1}{2}$" lengths for the side borders.

BLOCK ASSEMBLY
1. **Set A:** Sew five strips together in this order: white-red-white-red-white. Make 5 strip sets for 30 triangles.
Set B: Sew strips together in the opposite order: red-white-red-white-red. Make 5 strip sets for 30 triangles.

Press the white strips toward the red strips so the red doesn't show through.

To avoid stretching the strip sets, use spray starch on the wrong side and gently press them before cutting into triangles.

2. To cut the stripped triangles, line up the 45° angle line of your acrylic ruler with the base of the first strip in the strip set as shown below.

Strip Set A

Strip Set B

Make the first cut, then rotate your ruler, placing the 45° angle line of the ruler at the top of the strip and line up the edge of the ruler with the point of the triangle. Make the second cut to complete one triangle.

Rotate the ruler again so the 45° angle line is at the base of the first strip and the edge of the ruler is at the point of the triangle and cut.

3. Sew each stripped triangle to a blue triangle. Carefully press the seam toward the blue triangle. Trim if needed for a 7½" unfinished block.

Block A

Block B

QUILT ASSEMBLY

1. Arrange your blocks on a design wall (it can be as simple as a flannel-backed tablecloth pinned to the wall) according to the quilt assembly diagram.

2. Join the blocks together in A/B pairs. Press seams toward A block. Join pairs together in sets of 4 blocks. Press seams of alternate sets in opposite directions so when sewing block sets into rows, the seams nest together.

3. Sew the four block units together into rows. Press seams of alternate rows in opposite directions.

4. Join rows together. Press seams in one direction.

5. For each border, pin and then sew the top and bottom border lengths, press toward the border. Add

the side borders, press toward the border.

QUILTING

The quiltmaker machine quilted a small stipple stitch in the red strips, which effectively helps to make the white strips pop out. A larger, meandering stipple stitch was used in all other areas of the quilt, with the exception of the third medium blue border, where a continuous loop design of various sizes was quilted.

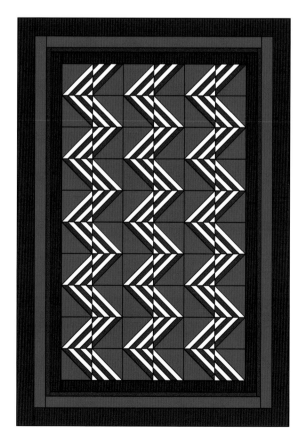

Quilt Assembly

16" square finished, machine pieced by Michele Y. Crawford.

FABRIC REQUIREMENTS

Red: $1/8$ yard or scraps
Medium Blue: $1/2$ yard (includes pillow backing)
Dark Blue: $1/4$ yard or scraps
White for piping: $1/2$ yard
16" pillow form
$1/4$" **cording for piping:** 2 yards

CUTTING

Red:

Cut four $3^3/8$" squares. Cut in half diagonally to make half-square triangles (A). You will need 7 triangles.

Medium Blue:

Cut four $3^3/8$" squares. Cut in half diagonally to make half-square triangles (B). You will need 7 triangles.

- Cut two $2^3/4$" squares (C).
- Cut two 3" squares (D).
- Cut two $1^5/8$" x $12^1/2$" rectangles (E).
- Cut two $2^3/4$" x 8" rectangles (F).

Dark Blue:

Cut one $2^3/4$" x $12^1/2$" rectangle (G).

BORDERS

Dark Blue:

Cut four $2^1/2$" x $12^1/2$" rectangles.

Medium Blue:

Cut four $2^1/2$" squares for corner posts.

PIPING

Cut bias strips $1^5/8$" wide from white fabric.

PILLOW BACK

Medium Blue:

Cut two 10" x $16^1/2$" rectangles.

PILLOW ASSEMBLY

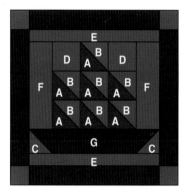

1. Sew together seven pairs of red A and medium blue B half-square triangles. Press toward blue B triangles. Arrange half-square triangle units and blue D squares as shown in horizontal rows. Sew horizontal rows together. Press seams of alternate rows in opposite directions. Add the F rectangles to both sides of the combined rows. Press toward the rectangles.

2. To create the boat base, attach a $2^3/4$" C square to opposite corners of the

$2^3/_4$" x $12^1/_2$" G rectangle by sewing on the diagonal. It helps to first finger-press the square diagonally in half to form a sewing guideline. Trim the extra fabric to a $^1/_4$" seam allowance and press toward the triangle as indicated.

3. Sew the boat base unit to the pieced sail unit. Press seam toward the boat.

4. Sew the top and bottom medium blue E rectangles to the sailboat unit. Press seam toward E.

5. Add the top and bottom dark blue border strips. Press seam toward the border.

6. Sew the medium blue corner posts to the ends of the dark blue side-border strips. Press seam toward the border strip. Add to the block. Press seam toward the border.

7. **Piping:** Sew bias strips together at a right angle; press seam open. You could also make a continuous bias strip following directions in most how-to-sew books.

You will need a continuous strip that is approximately 70" long. Place the cording in the center of the wrong side of the bias casing, and fold casing over the cord. Using a longer stitch and your zipper foot, sew the cording into the casing by stitching close to the cord. Matching raw edges, pin the cording to the edge of the pieced pillow top. Sew to top using a zipper foot. Stop stitching when you are about $1^1/_2$" away from the first end of the cording and leave the needle in the fabric. Trim the second cording end so it will overlap the first end by about $1^1/_2$". Pull out and trim $^3/_4$" of cord from each end. With both ends extending into the seam allowance, cross the empty casing and finish stitching the cording to the pillow top.

8. **Backing:** Two overlapping pieces are used for the pillow backing (dark blue was used for our pillow). To form finished edges on each backing piece, turn under and press $^1/_4$" along one $16^1/_2$" edge. Then turn under an additional $^1/_4$" and topstitch the edge.

9. Overlap the two pieces, centering the two folded edges, to create a $16^1/_2$"

square. Pin at the center to temporarily hold the two sides together.

10. Place the back right sides together with the pillow top, and remove the pins from Step 9. Pin around all sides.

11. Using a $^1/_4$" seam allowance, sew around all of the edges.

12. Trim the corners, and turn inside out. Press.

13. Insert the pillow form.

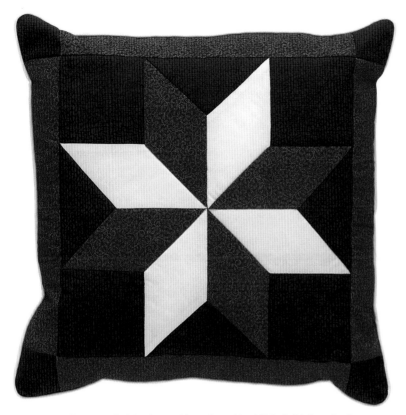

16" square finished, machine pieced by Michele Y. Crawford.

FABRIC REQUIREMENTS

Red: $^5/_8$ yard

Dark Blue: $^1/_3$ yard

White: $^5/_8$ yard

16" pillow form

$^1/_4$" cording for piping:
2 yards

CUTTING

Rotary cut the diamonds or use the template on page 53.

White (A):

Cut one 3"-wide strip. Make a 45° cut on one end of the strip. Move your ruler along the strip so the 3" line is on the previous cut and the 45° line of the ruler is aligned with the horizontal edge of the strip. Cut. Repeat for a total of 4 white diamonds.

Red (B):

Repeat the cutting instructions for the white diamonds above for a total of 4 red diamonds.

Dark Blue:

Cut four 4" squares (D). Cut one 6 $^1/_4$" square, then cut in half diagonally twice to make quarter-square triangles (C).

BORDERS
Red:

Cut four 2$^1/_2$" x 12" rectangles.

Dark Blue:

Cut four 2$^1/_2$" squares for corner posts.

PIPING

Cut bias strips 1$^5/_8$" wide from white fabric.

PILLOW BACK
Red:

Cut two 10 x 16$^1/_2$" rectangles.

PILLOW ASSEMBLY

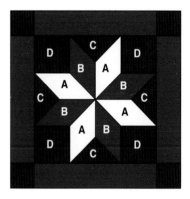

1. Mark a dot $^1/_4$" in from the corner of the C triangles, and the D squares on the wrong side of the fabric. This is the start and stop point of the Y seam.

2. It is helpful to lay the pieces out for each block. Make four units as shown. Sew in the direction of the arrows, backstitching at the dot.

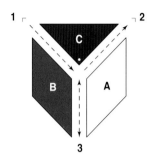

Seam 3 can be sewn in either direction.

3. Press as indicated.

Press open

4. Sew a D square to each red/white unit as indicated. Backstitch at the dot. Press as indicated.

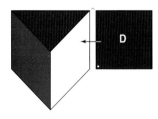

5. Sew two units together to create half of the block. Sew in the direction of the arrows and press as indicated.

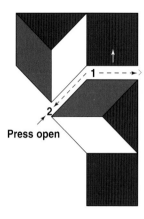

Press open

6. Sew two halves together to complete the LeMoyne star block. Sew in the direction of the arrows and press as indicated.

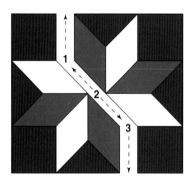

Press center seam open.

7. Add the top and bottom red border strips. Press seams toward the border.

8. Sew a dark blue corner post to the ends of the red side-border strips. Add to the block. Press seam toward the border strip.

9. **Piping:** Sew bias strips together at a right angle; press seam open. You could also make a continuous bias strip following directions in most how-to-sew books.

You will need a continuous strip that is approximately 70" long. Place the cording in the center of the wrong side of the bias casing, and fold casing over the cord. Using a longer stitch and your zipper foot, sew the cording into the casing by stitching close to the cord. With raw edges together, pin the cording to the edge of the pieced pillow top. Sew to top using a zipper foot.

Stop stitching when you are about 1^1/$_2$" away from the first end of the cording and leave the needle in the fabric. Trim the second cording end so it will overlap the first end by about 1^1/$_2$". Pull out and trim ^{3}/$_4$" of cord from each end.

With both ends extending into the seam allowance, cross the empty casing and finish stitching the cording to the pillow top.

10. **Backing:** Two overlapping pieces are used for the pillow backing (dark blue was used for our pillow). To form finished edges on each backing piece, turn under and press $1/4$" along one $16^1/_2$" edge. Then turn under an additional $1/4$" and topstitch the edge.

11. Overlap the two pieces, centering the two folded edges, to create a $16^1/_2$" square. Pin at the center to temporarily hold the two sides together.

12. Place the back right sides together with the pillow top, and remove the pins from Step 11. Pin around all sides.

13. Using a $1/4$" seam allowance, sew around all of the edges.

14. Trim the corners, and turn inside out. Press.

15. Insert the pillow form.

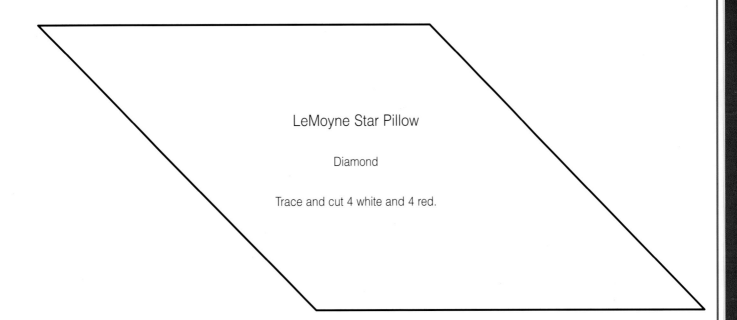

LeMoyne Star Pillow

Diamond

Trace and cut 4 white and 4 red.

A U T U M N

The sun is lower in the sky and the days grow shorter, the nights chillier. Cool evenings and frosty mornings begin to replace the warm summer days. The garden has past its peak. Pantry shelves are filled with jars of canned vegetables, fruits, and jellies. Autumn has arrived in a blaze of color that even my paintbrush struggles to fully capture. Autumn is my favorite time of year. No other season fills me with such joy and happiness.

◀ *Autumn Joy*

When I lived back east, I enjoyed many long drives and walks in the Pocono Mountains of Pennsylvania. Rolling hills and farmland were filled with color after color: golds, yellows, oranges, reds, and russets. On a sunny autumn afternoon, sunlight washes the picturesque covered bridges, white-steepled churches, and red barns, giving the leaves luminous, iridescent hues.

I love walking down a country road, the colorful leaves dancing and swirling around me. The leaves crunch underfoot; I inhale the muskiness of the autumn leaves and feel the brisk chill of the cooler air.

The old-time country store is a favorite painting subject. In *Autumn Joy* (page 54), the pumpkins ripen in the farmer's field while apples fall from the apple trees to fill waiting baskets. On a crisp autumn day under blue skies, a group of quilters

gathers to sit and quilt beneath the apple tree and catch up on the local news. Inside the country store, a fire burns in the old wood stove, and the scent of warm apple cider with cinnamon sticks drifts through the air.

Colors of autumn.

Maple Leaf Quilt and Table Runner

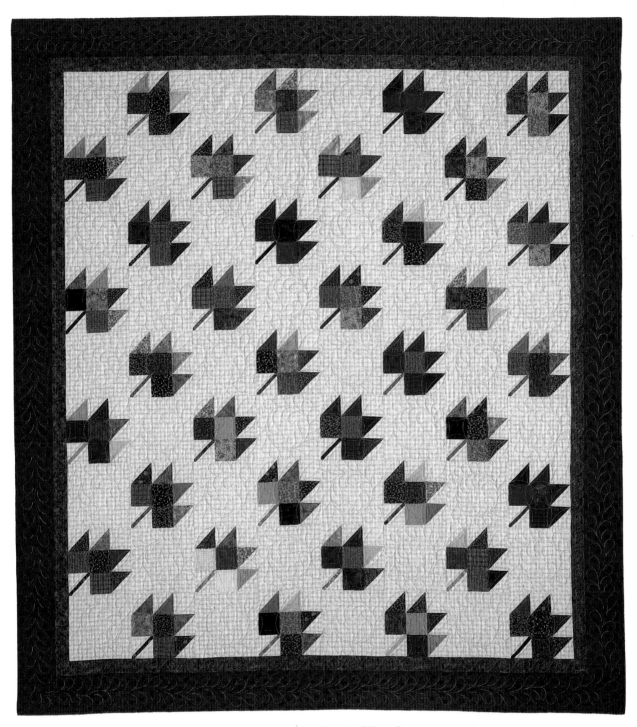

Machine pieced and quilted by Tiffany Burrow.

The quilt shown here follows the scrappy color scheme of the Maple Leaf quilt shown in Diane's autumn scene on page 54: reds, red-oranges, yellows, golds, browns, burgundies, rusts, and browns. You can follow her lead or choose colors of the other seasons: the greens of early spring, hot summertime brights, or wintery blues, whites, and silvers.

◀ *Oley Farm in Autumn*

FINISHED PROJECT SIZES

Lap–Size Quilt: 68$^1/_2$" x 50$^1/_2$"

Twelve 9" finished Maple Leaf Blocks with twelve 9" alternate plain blocks

Blocks set: 4 x 6 blocks

Double-bed Size Quilt: 86$^1/_2$" x 95$^1/_2$"

Thirty-six 9" finished Maple Leaf blocks with thirty-six 9" alternate plain blocks

Blocks Set: 8 x 9 blocks

Table Runner: 59$^1/_2$" x 16$^1/_2$"

Six 6" blocks (length can be adjusted by adding or subtracting blocks or borders)

Fabrics for the quilt shown on page 59 and 63 were graciously donated by Benartex Inc. from their Harvest Home and Color Reference Library Collections. Thread was donated by Coats and Clark.

FABRIC REQUIREMENTS

	Lap Quilt	Double-Bed Quilt	Table Runner
Background	1$^5/_8$ yards (includes alternate plain blocks)	4 yards (includes alternate plain blocks)	$^5/_8$ yard (includes corner and setting triangles)
Leaves	1 yard assorted fabrics	2$^1/_4$ yards assorted fabrics*	$^1/_2$ yard assorted fabrics
Inner Border**	$^1/_2$ yard	$^2/_3$ yard	$^1/_4$ yard
Outer Border**	1$^1/_8$ yards	1$^1/_2$ yards	$^1/_2$ yard
Backing	3 yards	7$^1/_2$ yards	1 yard
Batting	72" x 54"	90" x 99"	20" x 63"
Binding	$^1/_2$ yard	$^2/_3$ yard	$^1/_3$ yard

* For the quilt pictured, thirty-five $^1/_8$" yard cuts of fabrics from Benartex's Harvest Home and Color Reference Library fabric lines were used.

** Leftover yardage can be used for some of the leaves.

CUTTING

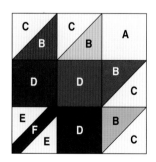

BACKGROUND

(A) Squares

Lap Quilt: Cut one 3$^1/_2$"-wide strip into twelve 3$^1/_2$" squares.

Double-Bed Quilt: Cut three 3$^1/_2$"-wide strips into thirty-six 3$^1/_2$" squares. *If fabric width is less than 42" wide, cut another 3$^1/_2$"-wide strip.*

Table Runner: Cut six 2$^1/_2$" squares.

Half-Square Triangles (C)

Lap Quilt: Cut three 3$^7/_8$"-wide strips into twenty-four 3$^7/_8$" squares. Cut squares in half diagonally for 48 triangles.

Double-Bed Quilt: Cut eight 3$^7/_8$"-wide strips into seventy-two 3$^7/_8$" squares. Cut squares in half diagonally for 144 triangles.

Table Runner: Cut one 2$^7/_8$"-wide strip into twelve 2$^7/_8$" squares. Cut squares in half diagonally for 24 triangles.

Half-Square Triangles for Stem (E)

Lap Quilt: Cut two 3$^5/_8$"-wide strips into twelve 3$^5/_8$" squares. Cut squares in half diagonally for 24 triangles.

Double-Bed Quilt: Cut four $3^5/_8$"-wide strips into thirty-six $3^5/_8$" squares. Cut squares in half diagonally for 72 triangles.

Table Runner: Cut six $2^5/_8$" squares, then cut squares diagonally for 12 triangles.

ALTERNATE PLAIN BLOCKS

Lap Quilt: Cut three $9^1/_2$"-wide strips into twelve $9^1/_2$" squares.

Double-Bed Quilt: Cut nine $9^1/_2$"-wide strips into thirty-six $9^1/_2$" squares.

Corner and Setting Triangles for Table Runner:

Cut one $9^3/_4$"-wide strip into three $9^3/_4$" squares and two $5^1/_8$" squares. Cut the $9^3/_4$" squares in half diagonally twice. You will need 10 quarter-square setting triangles. Cut the $5^1/_8$" squares in half diagonally once. You will need 4 half-square corner triangles.

LEAVES

Half-Square Triangles (B)

Lap Quilt: Cut two to three $3^7/_8$" squares from each fabric. You will need a total of 24 squares. Cut the squares in half diagonally for 48 triangles.

Double-Bed Quilt: Cut three to five $3^7/_8$"-wide squares from each fabric. You will need a total of 72 squares. Cut the

squares in half diagonally for 144 half-square triangles.

Table Runner: Cut two $2^7/_8$"-wide squares from a variety of fabrics for each block for a total of 12 squares. Cut the squares in half diagonally for 24 triangles.

Squares (D)

Lap Quilt: Cut three to five $3^1/_2$" squares from different fabrics. You will need 36 squares.

Double-Bed Quilt: Cut four to seven $3^1/_2$" squares from 8-12 fabrics. You will need 108 squares.

Table Runner: Cut three $2^1/_2$" squares per block from an assortment of fabrics. Need a total of 18 squares.

(F) Stem Strips: Cut 1" strips about 6" long for individual blocks. Cut the strips longer if making more than one block from the same fabric.

BORDERS

Before you cut the borders, follow the instructions in the General Guidelines (page 102), and check the final measurements of your quilt top. Adjust the border cutting lengths if necessary.

INNER BORDER

Lap Quilt: Cut five $2^1/_2$"-wide strips. Sew together end to end with diagonal seams. Then cut

two $54^1/_2$" lengths for side borders and two $40^1/_2$" lengths for the top and bottom borders.

Double-Bed Quilt: Cut eight $2^1/_2$"-wide strips. Sew together end to end with diagonal seams. Then cut two $81^1/_2$" lengths for side borders and two $76^1/_2$" lengths for top and bottom borders.

Table Runner: Cut four $1^1/_2$"-wide strips. Sew pairs of strips together end to end with diagonal seams. Then cut a 9" length for each side border and a $53^1/_2$" length for top or bottom border from each pair.

OUTER BORDER

Lap Quilt: Cut six $5^1/_2$"-wide strips. Sew together end to end with diagonal seams. Then cut two $58^1/_2$" lengths for side borders and two $50^1/_2$" lengths for the top and bottom borders.

Double-Bed Quilt: Cut nine $5^1/_2$"-wide strips. Sew together end to end with diagonal seams. Then cut two $85^1/_2$" lengths for side borders and two $86^1/_2$" lengths for top and bottom borders.

Table Runner: Cut four $3^1/_2$"-wide strips. Sew pairs together end to end with diagonal seams. Then cut an 11" length for side borders and a $59^1/_2$"

length for top and bottom border from each pair.

BLOCK ASSEMBLY

1. For each block sew four half-square triangle units (B/C), right sides together. Press seam toward the B triangle.

2. To make the stem squares sew an E triangle to each side of the F stem strip. Press the seams toward the stem strips. Trim the unit to 3½" square for quilts. Trim the unit to 2½" square for the table runner.

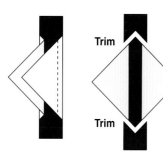

3. Arrange and sew the block into rows. Press seams of alternate rows in opposite directions. The block should measure 9½" square for the quilts, 6½" square for the table runner.

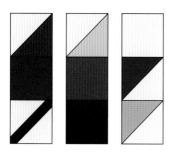

Quilt Assembly

Table Runner Assembly

QUILT ASSEMBLY

1. Arrange the blocks in the order shown, alternating the Maple Leaf blocks with the plain background squares. *Tip: Before you sew the blocks together, mark your chosen quilting design on the plain background squares.*

2. Sew the blocks together into horizontal rows. Press the seams toward the plain squares. Sew the rows together. Press the seams in one direction.

3. Add the inner side borders to the quilt top first. Press the seams toward the border. Then add the inner top and bottom borders. Press seams toward the border. Repeat for the outer borders.

QUILTING

As noted in the tip above, the quiltmaker marked a feather wreath design on the alternate plain blocks before the blocks were sewn together to make the quilt top. If you choose to machine quilt, secure the layers first by stitching in-the-ditch along the center horizontal and vertical rows. Moving from the center out, stitch-in-the-ditch in all horizontal and vertical rows. Machine quilt the wreaths in each plain block.

TABLE RUNNER ASSEMBLY

1. Arrange the blocks and setting triangles in the order shown. Sew together in diagonal rows. Press the seams toward the setting triangles and corner squares.

2. Add borders as in Step 3 of Quilt Assembly.

3. Finish following General Guidelines. Quilt as desired.

Autumn One-Patch Quilt

Machine pieced and quilted by Tiffany Burrow.

To celebrate this colorful season, look for autumnal tone-on-tone prints to follow Diane's lead on page 54.
As a crib quilt, this would also be wonderful in vivid brights, juvenile novelty prints, or pastels
(as illustrated in the diagram on page 65).

Finished Quilt Size:

$45^{3}/_{8}$" x 54"

FABRIC REQUIREMENTS

(Numbers relate to Strip Set Construction)

Fabric 1 (Maize):

$^{1}/_{4}$ yard

Fabric 2 (Red Brown):

$^{1}/_{3}$ yard

Fabric 3 (Dark Purple):

$^{1}/_{4}$ yard

Fabric 4 (Medium Blue):

$^{1}/_{3}$ yard

Fabric 5 (Orange):

$^{1}/_{4}$ yard

Fabric 6 (Light Green):

$^{1}/_{3}$ yard

Fabric 7 (Lilac):

$^{1}/_{4}$ yard

Fabric 8 (Burgundy):

$^{2}/_{3}$ yard (includes Border 2)

Fabric 9 (Gold):

$^{1}/_{2}$ yard (includes Border 1)

Fabric 10 (Dark Green):

$1^{3}/_{8}$ yards (includes corner and setting triangles, Border 3, and binding)

Backing: 3 yards

Batting: 50" x 58"

CUTTING

STRIPS

Fabrics 1 through 8:

Cut two $2^{1}/_{2}$"-wide strips.

Fabric 9:

Cut one $2^{1}/_{2}$"-wide strip.

SETTING TRIANGLES

Fabrics 2, 4, 6, and 8:

Cut one $4^{1}/_{8}$" square from each. Cut squares in half diagonally twice.

Fabric 10:

Cut six $4^{1}/_{8}$" squares. Cut squares in half diagonally twice. You will need only 22 quarter-square triangles.

CORNER TRIANGLES

Fabric 10:

Cut two $2^{3}/_{8}$" squares. Cut squares diagonally in half in half once. The triangles will be slightly larger than needed; once they are sewn on you can square up the corners of the quilt.

BORDERS

Before you cut the borders, follow the instructions in the General Guidelines (page 102), and check the final measurements of your quilt top. Adjust the border cutting lengths if necessary.

Border 1 (Fabric 9, Gold):

Sides: Cut two strips $2^{1}/_{2}$" x 35".
Top and Bottom: Cut two strips $2^{1}/_{2}$" x $30^{3}/_{8}$".

Border 2 (Fabric 8, Burgundy):

Sides: Cut two strips $3^{1}/_{2}$" x 39".
Top and Bottom: Cut two strips $3^{1}/_{2}$" x $36^{3}/_{8}$".

Border 3 (Fabric 10, Dark Green):

Sides: Cut five 5"-wide strips. Sew together end to end with diagonal seams. Then cut two 45" lengths for side borders and two $45^{3}/_{8}$" lengths for top and bottom borders.

QUILT ASSEMBLY

1. Begin by sewing the following strips in sets in the order given below. Press the seams toward the odd-numbered fabrics (1, 3, 5, 7, and 9) so the seams nest together when sewing the rows to one another in Step 4.

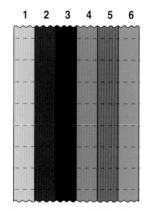

Make two sets of Strip Set 1.

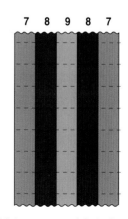

Make one set of Strip Set 2.

2. Cut each strip set into 2½" units. You need 26 units from Strip Set 1 and 12 units from Strip Set 2.

3. Lay out the strip units and setting triangles in diagonal rows according to the assembly diagram on a design wall or piece of batting pinned to a wall. For partial strips you will need to remove some squares. Save two removed Fabric 1 squares for the first and last row. Save two Fabric 7 squares for Rows 4 and 17.

4. Sew triangles and strip units together in diagonal rows, then sew the rows together. Add the four corner triangles to finish the top. Check and trim the corners using a square acrylic ruler.

5. Pin and stitch the first side borders to the quilt top. Press seams toward the border. Pin and stitch the top and bottom borders to the quilt top. Press seams toward the border.

6. Repeat Step 5 for the second and third borders.

QUILTING

The quiltmaker stitched in-the-ditch around the pieced center, and around each border. She then quilted an overall grid through the center of each on-point square. A different quilting design was used in each border.

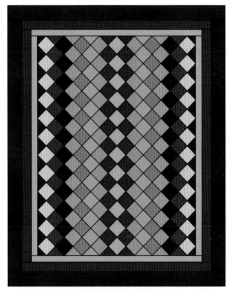

Add borders

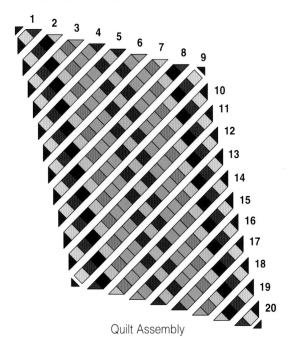

Quilt Assembly

This variation on the color scheme would make a wonderful crib quilt or spring wallhanging.

W * I * N * T * E * R

In Pennsylvania, the sleeping ground and dormant trees often rest beneath a white "quilt" of snow. The landscape looks so beautiful. While the snow is falling, there is a quiet stillness and a wonderfully fresh, crisp smell in the air. Autumn is my favorite season for its wonderful color and brightness, but winter is my second favorite for its simplicity. The trees are bare, the busyness of the leaves are gone. I love painting the branches and being able to see the structure of the tree. Snow-covered landscapes are so peaceful and serene.

◀ *Amish Winter*

Many of my fondest memories are of the snow: ice-skating on a frozen pond while burning logs snap and crackle nearby, where you can warm up with a cup of hot chocolate. In past winters, I have gone on snow-covered hikes at Lake Tahoe in California and the Grand Canyon in Arizona, as well as countless walks down the country lanes of Pennsylvania.

▼ *Skaters' Bonfire*

Another very special place is Mt. Hood, Oregon, part of the Cascade Range, about an hour's drive from Portland, Oregon. At the very top of this gorgeous mountain is a resort called the Timberline Lodge, a magnificent treasure built during the Depression. The lodge and guest rooms are decorated throughout with original woodcarvings and artwork. We like to stay there during the Christmas holidays, when it is beautifully decorated. From the top of Mt. Hood

you can see for many miles and can spot the other Cascade Mountain peaks, including the Three Sisters (named Hope, Faith, and Charity), as well as Mt. Adams, Mt. Jefferson, and Mt. St. Helens. Breathtaking!

There is something magical and quite wonderful about snowy nights. I love when a full moon's brightness casts wonderful shadows on the snow. The moonlit areas sparkle like diamonds.

In the winter months, the pace slows. The Amish lifestyle, especially, reflects this slower time. The work of the spring and summer planting is finished. Pantries bulge with the labors of the harvest. While the family gathers indoors, many Amish women find time to quilt during long winter evenings. The snow blows and drifts to cover the bare fields, but everyone is warm and toasty by the wood stove in the kitchen.

In *Amish Winter* (page 66), the old-order Amish homestead is peaceful and serene. Nearby chickadees sing and call to each other. An early morning between snowstorms finds the wash-line in use. Quilts are airing and will smell crisp and clean when they are warming the bed tonight. Every Amish buggy has a quilt inside for warmth on those cold winter drives. When the snow becomes impassable by buggy, the sleigh and horses can be seen travel-ing the backroads.

◄ *Stout Valley, Pennsylvania, Schoolhouse*

Snowflake Quilt

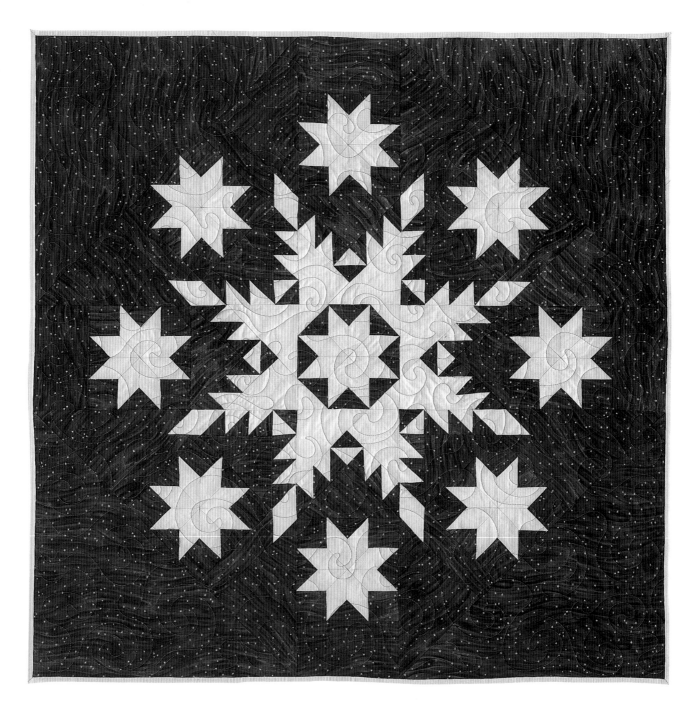

Machine pieced by Joyce Lytle, machine quilted by Laura Lee Fritz.

A whimsical navy print contrasts with a light violet background. Although the print is directional, we chose to rotary cut the block pieces. Cutting the pieces so they would all be "headed in the same direction" would require more yardage.

SNOWFLAKE QUILT

Fabrics for the quilt shown were graciously donated by Robert Kaufman Fine Fabrics from the Kona Cotton and Jennifer Sampou's Designer Essentials collection. Thread was donated by Coats and Clark.

Finished Quilt Size: 40" square

Block size: 6³/₈" square

Please Note: This project would be a challenge for the beginning quilter.

FABRIC REQUIREMENTS

Light color: ⁷/₈ yard

Dark color: 1³/₄ yards

Backing: 1¹/₄ yards (If your fabric is less than 44"-wide, purchase more fabric so a strip can be added to increase width of backing.)

Binding: ³/₈ yard

Batting: 45" x 45"

CUTTING

LIGHT COLOR

Diamonds (A): Cut six 1¹³/₁₆"-wide strips. (Line up your ruler so the edge of the fabric is halfway between the 1³/₄" and 1⁷/₈" lines on

the ruler.) Then position the 45° line of the ruler on the fabric's edge and cut one end of the strip. Keeping the 45° line on the fabric's edge, slide the ruler over 1¹³/₁₆" and cut. Remember this width is between the parallel lines of the ruler. Repeat until you have 72 diamonds. Or make a template from the pattern provided on page 106, and cut 72 diamonds.

Cutting Diamonds

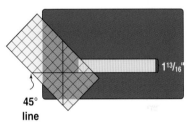

Cut end of strip at 45° angle.

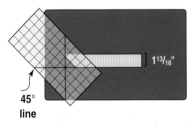

Slide ruler over 1¹³/₁₆" and cut.

Half-Square Triangles (E):

After cutting F and G, cut two 2³/₄" squares from left over 5³/₈"-wide strip. Then cut the squares diagonally once.

Triangles (F) and Kites (G):

Cut one 5³/₈"-wide strip into

four 5 3/8" squares. Then cut the squares diagonally once. Four of the triangles are (F). Cut the remaining four triangles into kite shapes (G) by placing the 5 3/8" line of the ruler at the tip of the triangle and the end of the ruler on the long bias edge of the triangle. Cut off the excess triangle fabric.

Cutting kite shapes from half-square triangles.

Half-Square Triangles (I):

Cut two 2 3/8"-wide strips into twenty 2 3/8" squares. Then cut the squares diagonally once.

Diamonds (J):

Cut one 2"-wide strip. Then position the 45° line of the ruler on the fabric's edge and cut one end of the strip. Keeping the 45° line on the fabric's edge, slide the ruler over 2" and cut. Repeat until you have 8 diamonds. Or make a template from the (J) diamond pattern on page 106, and cut 8 diamonds.

DARK COLOR

Quarter-Square Triangles (B):

Cut one 3 7/8"-wide strip into nine 3 7/8" squares. Then cut the squares diagonally twice.

Squares (C): Cut two 2 3/8"-wide strips into thirty-two 2 3/8" squares.

Half-Square Triangles (D):

After cutting K, cut two 2 3/4" squares from the leftover 5 3/8"-wide strip. Then cut the squares diagonally once.

Half-Square Triangles (H):

Cut two 2 3/8"-wide strips into twenty-eight 2 3/8" squares. Then cut the squares diagonally once.

Large Triangles (K): Cut one 5 3/8"-wide strip into four 5 3/8" squares. Then cut the squares diagonally once.

Rectangles (L): Cut one 4"-wide strip. From the strip into four 4" x 6 7/8" rectangles.

Half Trapezoids (M): Cut two 2"-wide strips. Place the strips wrong-sides together and cut four 7 1/4" lengths. Then from one lower corner of the rectangle, place the 45° line of the ruler on the long edge rectangle. Cut the triangle(s) off. You will have

four left half-trapezoids and four right half-trapezoids.

Cutting Half Trapezoids

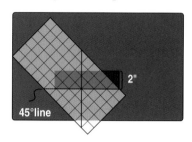

With 7 1/4" rectangles wrong sides together, cut end of rectangle at 45° angle.

Setting Triangles (N): Cut one 7 7/8"-wide strip into four 7 7/8" squares. Then cut the squares diagonally once.

Corner Triangles (O): Cut one 17 3/8"-wide strip into two 17 3/8" squares. Then cut the squares diagonally once.

ASSEMBLY OF LEMOYNE STAR BLOCKS

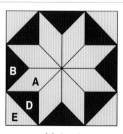

Make 1

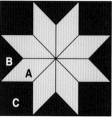

Make 8

You will need nine 6³⁄₈" finished LeMoyne Star blocks. Note that the center star's corners are half-square triangles (D and E) instead of dark squares (C).

1. Mark a dot ¼" in from the corner of the B and D triangles, and the C squares on the wrong side of the fabric. This is the start and stop point of the Y seam.

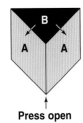

2. It helps to lay the pieces out for each block. Make four Unit 1's as shown for each block. Sew in the direction of the arrows, backstitching at the dot.

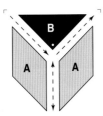

Seam 3 can be sewn in either direction

Unit 1—Make 4 for each star for a total of 36 Unit 1's.

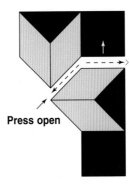

Press open

3. Press as indicated.

4. For the center star, sew four D/E units. Press as indicated.

5. Sew a D/E unit to each Unit 1 creating Unit 2 for the center star. Sew a C square to each Unit 1 for the other eight stars. Backstitch at the dot. Press as indicated.

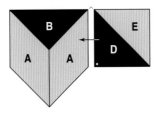

Unit 2

6. Sew two Unit 2's together, creating Unit 3. Sew in the direction of the arrows and press as indicated.

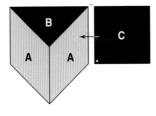

Press open

Unit 3

7. Sew two unit 3's together creating the LeMoyne star block. Sew in the direction of the arrows and press as indicated.

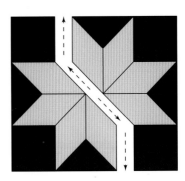

Press center seam open.

SAWTOOTH UNITS ASSEMBLY

1. Chain sew 40 light (I) and 40 dark (H) half-square triangle units together. Press seam toward the dark triangle.

2. Sew together pairs of half-square triangle squares to make 8 sawtooth units and 8 mirror-image sawtooth units. Press seam toward the dark triangle.

Make 8 Sawtooth Units.

Make 8 mirror-image Sawtooth Units.

75

3. Add a J diamond to eight dark (H) triangles. Press seam toward the diamond.

4. Add H/J units to 8 of the Sawtooth units. Press seam toward the dark triangle. Save these J-Sawtooth units for the corner units of the side sections.

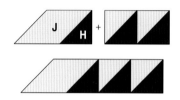

Make 4 J-Sawtooth units.

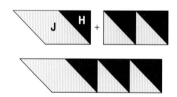

Make 4 mirror-image J-Sawtooth units.

5. Add an H triangle to the other 8 Sawtooth units. Press seam toward the dark triangle.

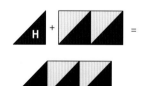

Make 4 H-Sawtooth units.

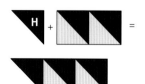

.Make 4 mirror-image H-Sawtooth units

QUILT ASSEMBLY

1. It is easier to make the quilt in sections. Arrange all the pieces on a design board.

2. Make 4 middle units, two for the center section and two for the side sections. Stitch one H-Sawtooth unit to one side of the dark half-square triangle (K). Press seam toward the K triangle.

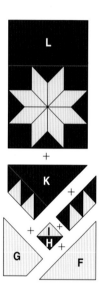

Make four Middle Units.

3. Sew an H/I half-square triangle unit to the end of a H-Sawtooth unit. Press seam toward the light triangle. Join this to the unit created in the previous step.

4. Sew a kite (G) to the unit created in Step 3. Then add an F triangle to other side. Press seams toward kite (G) and triangle (F). Add this unit

to one side of a LeMoyne Star block. Press seam toward K.

5. Sew L to opposite side of the LeMoyne Star. Press seam toward L.

6. To make the center section, join a middle unit to the center LeMoyne Star to a middle unit. Press seam toward F/G.

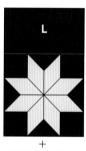

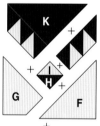

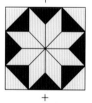

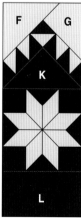

Center Section

7. Make four corner units for the side sections. Sew M to each side of a LeMoyne star. Press seams toward M.

8. Sew K to M/star/M unit. Press toward K.

9. Sew a J-Sawtooth unit (made in Step 4 of Sawtooth construction) to K/M/star/M unit. Press seam toward K/M.

10. Sew an H/I half-square unit to end of a J-Sawtooth unit. Press seam toward the light triangle. Join this to the other side of K/M/Star/M unit. Press toward K/M.

11. Sew an N triangle to each side. Press toward N.

12. Add an O triangle. Press toward O.

Make 4 Corner Units.

13. To make the side sections, sew a corner unit to a middle unit to a corner unit. Press seams open.

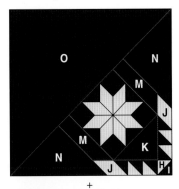

+

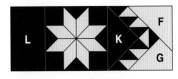

+

Side Sections

14. Join the side sections to the center section to complete the quilt top.

QUILTING

The quilter machine quilted a very effective overall swirling design to create the feel of a blustery snowstorm.

Log Cabin Star Quilt

Machine pieced and quilted by Barbara Baker.

This beautiful reproduction of Diane's Log Cabin Star Quilt (page 66) was created using a
variety of tone-on-tone prints in pinks, violets, purples, greens, and aquas in a range of values
from light to medium dark; two different yellows create the stars.

Fabrics for the quilt shown were graciously donated by P&B Textiles from their New Basics Color Collection. Thread was donated by Coats and Clark.

Finished Size: 90" x 114$\frac{1}{2}$"
Block Size: 12$\frac{1}{4}$" block finished
Blocks Set: 6 x 8

FABRIC REQUIREMENTS

Light Pink: $\frac{1}{2}$ yard
Medium Pink: $\frac{1}{2}$ yard
Dark Pink: $\frac{5}{8}$ yard
Magenta: 1 yard
Light Violet: $\frac{1}{2}$ yard
Medium Violet: $\frac{1}{2}$ yard
Dark Violet: $\frac{5}{8}$ yard
Purple: 3$\frac{1}{8}$ yards total:
$\frac{3}{8}$ yard for Log Cabin blocks, 2 yards for Outer Border, and $\frac{3}{4}$ yard for Binding

Light Green: $\frac{1}{2}$ yard
Medium Green: $\frac{3}{4}$ yard
Dark Green: 1 yard
Light Aqua: $\frac{5}{8}$ yard
Medium Aqua: $\frac{5}{8}$ yard
Dark Aqua: 1$\frac{3}{8}$ yards total:
$\frac{5}{8}$ yard for Log Cabin blocks and $\frac{3}{4}$ yard for Inner Border

Light Yellow: $\frac{5}{8}$ yard
Golden Yellow: $\frac{1}{2}$ yard
Backing: 9 yards
Batting: 94" x 118"

CUTTING
LOG CABIN BLOCKS
Cut 2$\frac{1}{4}$"-wide strips from each of the following fabrics.

Light Pink: 7 strips
Medium Pink: 6 strips
Dark Pink: 8 strips
Magenta: 13 strips

Light Violet: 8 strips
Medium Violet: 5 strips
Dark Violet: 8 strips
Purple: 5 strips

Light Green: 6 strips
Medium Green: 10 strips
Dark Green: 12 strips
Light Aqua: 8 strips
Medium Aqua: 8 strips
Dark Aqua: 9 strips

Light Yellow: 7 strips
Golden Yellow: 5 strips

STAR POINTS
Subcut three of the **Golden Yellow** strips into forty-eight 2$\frac{1}{4}$" squares for the small star points.
Subcut five of the **Light Yellow** strips into forty-eight 2$\frac{1}{4}$" x 4" rectangles for the longer star points.

SAWTOOTH STARS
Light Yellow:
❋ Cut four 3$\frac{1}{2}$" squares for star centers.
❋ Cut one 2"-wide strip into sixteen 2" squares for star points.

Golden Yellow:
Cut one 2"-wide strip into sixteen 2" squares for star points.
Light Violet, Medium Green, Medium Aqua, and Medium Pink:
Cut four 2" x 3$\frac{1}{2}$" rectangles from each fabric.
Light Aqua, Dark Green, Dark Violet, and Magenta:
Cut four 2" squares from each fabric.

BORDERS
Before you cut the borders, follow the instructions in the General Guidelines (page 102), and check the final measurements of your quilt top. Adjust the border cutting lengths if necessary.

Inner Border (Dark Aqua):
Cut nine 2$\frac{1}{2}$"-wide strips. Sew together end to end with diagonal seams. Then cut two 98$\frac{1}{2}$" lengths for the side borders and two 78" lengths for the top and bottom borders.

Outer Border (Purple):
Cut ten 6$\frac{1}{2}$"-wide strips. Sew together end to end with diagonal seams. Then cut two 102$\frac{1}{2}$" lengths for the side borders and two 78" lengths for the top and bottom borders.

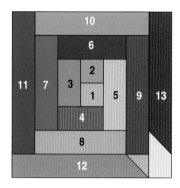

A block • Make 16

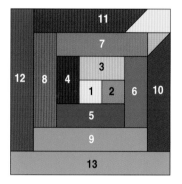

B block • Make 12

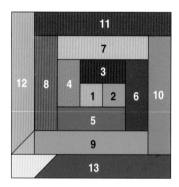

C block • Make 12

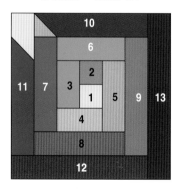

D block • Make 8

BLOCK ASSEMBLY

1. For the A and C blocks, make two strip sets with Golden Yellow and Light Green. Press the seam toward the green strip. Cut into 2¼" units for a total of 28 units. For the B and D blocks, make two strip sets with Light Yellow and Medium Green. Press the seam toward the green strip. Cut into 2¼" units for a total of 20 units.

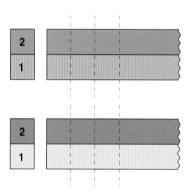

Strip sets for Log Cabin Centers.

2. Following the block diagrams for each block, and with right sides together, sew the first strip to the center squares, making sure the green square is at the top. Trim the edge even with the unit formed by the two center squares. Press the seam toward the added strip.

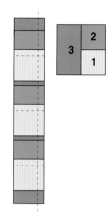

Adding the first long strip with center units on top.

3. Following the block diagrams, continue adding strips to the center unit, making sure the strip sewn on last is at the top of the block. You'll be turning the units in a clockwise direction to add the next strip to the left side of the unit. Sew the strips in the order shown in the block diagram. Trim, then press seams toward the added strip.

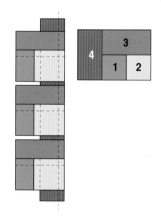

Adding the fourth color strip to the center unit.

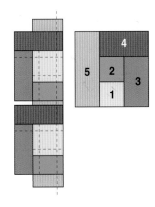

Adding the fifth color strip
to the center unit.

4. Notice that in Blocks A and C you need to treat the 12th and 13th strips–in Blocks B and D the 10th and 11th strips–a bit differently because you will be adding squares and rectangles for the star points.

Following the color sequencing in the block diagrams, first fold a Golden Yellow 2¼" square on the diagonal to form a stitching guideline. Place it on top of the 12th strip for Blocks A and C, the 10th strip for Blocks B and D, with right sides together. Stitch along the diagonal from corner to corner. Trim ¼" outside the seam line. Press the seam toward the longer strip.

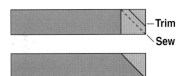

Adding Golden Yellow squares for the star points. Sew on the diagonal from corner to corner.

Next place a Light Yellow 2¼" x 4" rectangle on top of strip #13 for Blocks A and C, strip #11 for Blocks B and D. Stitch along the diagonal from corner to corner as shown. Trim ¼" outside the seam line. Press the seam toward the longer strip.

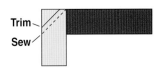

Adding Light Yellow rectangles for the star points. Sew on the diagonal from corner to corner.

5. Add these strips to the block according to the diagram for each block.

QUILT ASSEMBLY

1. Lay out the top two rows of blocks following the Quilt Assembly diagram on page 82. Although you are using just four different blocks, note how they are rotated within each row.

The first two rows are arranged in this order:

Row 1: A+C+A+A Rotated+B Rotated+A Rotated

Row 2: B+D+B+C Rotated+D Rotated+C Rotated

2. Pin the blocks together into rows, carefully matching the seams for the star points. Press the seams of alternating rows in opposite directions so when you pin the rows, the seams nest together. Sew the rows together. Press the seams in one direction.

3. Once you have sewn the first two rows together, you will follow the same block order, and sew three more identical pairs of rows.

4. Arrange your row sets as shown. Rows 3 and 4 are a repeat of Rows 1 and 2. Rows 5 and 6, 7 and 8 are also repeats of Rows 1 and 2, but the entire two rows are rotated 180° (upside down).

BORDERS

1. Follow the Assembly Diagram to add the borders. Pin and then sew the inner side border lengths, press the seam toward the border. Add the top and bottom borders,

press the seam toward the border.

2. Make four identical Sawtooth Star blocks. Sew the Light Yellow and Golden Yellow 2" squares to the 2" x 3½" rectangles as shown. Trim and press.

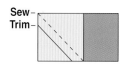

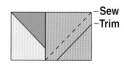

3. Sew the block together as shown. Press as indicated. Block should measure 6½" square.

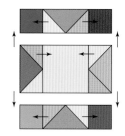

Make 4

4. Add the outer side border lengths. Press the seam toward the border.

5. Add a Sawtooth Star block to each end of the outer top and bottom borders. Press the seam toward the border strip.

6. Add the top and bottom borders. Press the seams toward the inner border.

QUILTING

The quiltmaker machine quilted a loose, overall meandering stipple design that features random stars. A star was quilted in each center yellow square of the Log Cabin blocks. Continuous-line larger stars were machine quilted in the outside border.

Quilt Assembly

A smaller quilt (90" x 65½") can be created by eliminating the two middle pairs of rows (rows 3 and 4, 5 and 6).

Enlarge to desired size.

C H R I S T M A S

Lighted candles, garlands of holly, fragrance of pine,

gaily wrapped gifts, and cheerful snowmen. Christmas time is

here! Christmas is a very special time of the year. Home

becomes the focal point during the holiday celebration. We

gather with family and friends at this time to enjoy the season.

We bundle up in mittens and scarves and go look for the special

Christmas tree. Everyone has treasured memories of this season

and cheerfully adds to them each year.

Christmas Cheer

In *Christmas Cheer* (page 84), I wanted to show the magic of the season. The holiday quilts are airing for family and friends who will sleep beneath their downy warmth on Christmas Eve. The snowman is attired in a quilted scarf, hat, mittens, and jacket. Cardinals and chickadees play on the bench and nearby fir trees. Lighted candles glow in the windows of the stone house and the barn boasts a Christmas wreath.

The stone house and old barn are very special to me. I have painted this homestead in different seasons and settings since I was a young girl. Pennsylvania is well-known for its many stone barns built with granite from Lehigh County (where I lived), gray limestone from nearby Bucks County, or red sandstone from Berks County. Stone barns have lasted in this area for over two centuries without showing any settling cracks. I just love the way they look! The stone portions of

Our Oregon backyard.

this painting took me the longest as each stone was painted individually.

Christmas Traditions

I started designing Christmas cards when I was about 15. My first design was of a Christmas tree with all the family names. My dad formed the sturdy trunk, my sisters (Linda, Mary, and Anne) and I were the evergreen branches, and my mom provided the star on top. For many years I drew each card one by one, graduating to a few years of silkscreen. Now I use reproductions of my watercolor paintings.

During the month of December I design and paint a new painting featuring Christmas quilts and memories; this design is used for the next year's card. This tradition always keeps me

▲ *Silent Night*

especially joyful during the holidays.

I grew up with many wonderful traditions during Christmas and New Year's. My mom and dad always made this a special time for our family. When the weather cooperated and we were blessed with a white Christmas, my sisters and I would spend the Christmas vacation building snow igloos and snowmen, as well as countless hours ice-skating and sleigh riding.

Christmas in Oregon

We have been very fortunate to have snow for Christmas a few times since our move to Oregon. When it snows, our home, woodlands, and creek are transformed into a winter wonderland. It is so beautiful. One year we were doubly blessed with snow and a full moon beneath a cloudless sky. The snow sparkled like diamonds and the trees made long shadows.

Mike and I both have families on the East Coast. Since we are unable to make it home every year, we have our own traditions, which are based on childhood memories. Our home is decorated throughout with candles, wreaths, and Christmas stockings for everyone, including our animal family.

One of the things we enjoy is searching for the perfect Christmas tree on the many tree farms in our area. We bake traditional cookies and goodies while listening to carols on the radio. Christmas morning finds us surrounded by gifts to each other and gifts from our families. We open them one by one and remember our families with each present we unwrap. Our golden retriever, Bogie, loves opening all her presents from Santa. She rips off the pretty paper to find new toys and rawhides to chew on. Socks and Gato watch Bogie but their gifts remain wrapped until "Mom" unwraps them.

Mike and I spend the afternoon talking on the phone with family and friends, thanking everyone for the wonderful gifts and making plans for the next annual visit back east in the spring. The rest of the day is spent cooking a traditional Christmas turkey dinner and counting our blessings!

Christmas Sampler Quilt

Machine pieced and quilted by Michele Y. Crawford.

Since this quilt uses two shades of red and two shades of green, try using a
bright red and a bright green to offset a darker red and green. A bright white
will lend a crisp feel to the overall appearance of the quilt.

Fabrics for the quilt shown were graciously donated by P&B Textiles from their Ramblings and New Basics collections. Thread was donated by Coats and Clark.

Finished Size: 38½" square
Block Size: 9" finished
Blocks Set: 3 x 3 with 1"-wide sashing and corner posts

FABRIC REQUIREMENTS

White: 1 yard
Medium red: ⅞ yard
Dark red: ¾ yard
Medium green: 1 yard (including binding)
Dark green: ¾ yard
Backing: 1¼ yards (purchase more if fabric width is less than 42" wide)
Batting: 42" square

CUTTING

WINDMILL BLOCK

Medium Red Large Triangles (A):
Cut two 5⅜"-wide strips into 8 squares. Cut each square diagonally in half.

Dark Green Triangles (B):
Cut one 5¾"-wide strip into 4 squares. Cut each square diagonally in half twice.

White Triangles (C):
Cut one 5¾"-wide strip into 4 squares. Cut each square diagonally in half twice.

VARIABLE STAR BLOCK

White Background (A & B):
Cut one 4¼"-wide strip into two 4¼" squares. Cut each square diagonally in half twice (A). Cut the remainder of the strip to 3½" wide. Cut into eight 3½" squares (B).

Dark Red Triangles (C):
Cut one 4¼"-wide strip into two 4¼" squares. Cut each square diagonally in half twice.

Dark Green Triangles (D):
Cut one 4¼"-wide strip into four 4¼" squares. Cut each square diagonally in half twice. From remainder of 4¼"-wide strip, cut two 3½" squares for the center of the blocks (E).

CORNER STAR BLOCK

Medium Red Squares (A):
Cut three 1⅝"-wide strips into sixty-four 1⅝" squares.

Dark Red Squares (B):
Cut one 2¾"-wide strip into ten 2¾" squares.

Dark Green Squares (C):
Cut one 2⅛" strip into 8 squares.

White Background (D & E):
Cut two 1⅝"-wide strips, then cut each strip into twelve 1⅝" x 2¾" rectangles (D) and four 1⅝" squares (E).

TREE BLOCK

White:
- Cut one 2½"-wide strip into six 2½" squares. Cut each diagonally in half for 12 triangles (A).
- Cut one 4¼"-wide strip and from that strip cut:
  One 4¼" square. Cut diagonally in half for B triangles.
  One 3½" square. Cut diagonally twice. Need only 1 (C) quarter-square triangle.
  One 2⅛" square (D)
  Two 2¾" x 3" rectangles (E)
  Two 1⅝" x 2" rectangles (F)
  Two 1½" x 1¾" rectangles (G)
  Two 1¾" squares (H)
  Two 2" squares. Cut each diagonally in half for I triangles.

Medium Red:
Cut one 3⅝"-wide strip (or use leftovers from other blocks), then cut one 3⅝" square and cut diagonally in half twice for J triangles. From remainder of the strip, cut one 1¾" x 4½" rectangle (K).

Dark Red:
From fabric left over from other blocks, cut one 3⅝" square. Cut diagonally in half twice. (Need three L triangles)

Medium Green:
From fabric left over from other blocks, cut two 3⅝" squares. Cut each diagonally

in half twice. (Need seven M triangles)

Dark Green:

Cut one $4\frac{1}{8}$"-wide strip, then cut one $4\frac{1}{8}$" square and cut diagonally in half. (Need one N triangle). From the remainder of the strip cut:

One $1\frac{5}{8}$" x 2" rectangle (O)

One $1\frac{1}{2}$" x 2" rectangle (P)

SASHING

Medium Green:

Cut six $1\frac{1}{2}$"-wide strips, then from two of the strips cut eight $9\frac{1}{2}$" lengths. From each of the four remaining strips cut one $29\frac{1}{2}$" length and one $9\frac{1}{2}$" length.

Dark Red:

Use leftover fabric or cut one $1\frac{1}{2}$" strip into eight $1\frac{1}{2}$" squares for the corner posts.

BORDERS

Before you cut the borders, follow the instructions in the General Guidelines (page 102), and check the final measurements of your quilt top. Adjust the border cutting lengths if necessary.

Inner White Border:

Cut two $1\frac{1}{2}$" x $31\frac{1}{2}$" strips for the top and bottom. Cut two $32\frac{1}{2}$" strips for the sides.

Outer Pieced Border:

Cut two $2\frac{1}{2}$"-wide strips of each color: medium red, dark red, medium green, and dark green. Cut one of the strips of each color in half (so you have 2 pieces, each about 20" long; you will only use one of the 20" pieces).

White Corner Half-Square Triangles: Cut two $3\frac{7}{8}$" squares. Cut each diagonally in half.

Dark Red Corner Half-Square Triangles: Cut two $3\frac{7}{8}$" squares. Cut each diagonally in half.

BLOCK ASSEMBLY
WINDMILL BLOCK

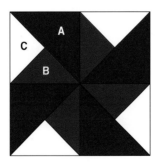

Make 4

1. Sew green triangles to white triangles. Press seam toward the green triangle.

2. Sew green/white unit to red triangle. Press seam toward the red triangle.

3. Sew four completed units together as shown to form block. Press.

VARIABLE STAR BLOCK

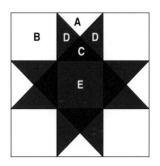

Make 2

1. Sew together pairs of white and green triangles. Press seam toward the green triangle.

2. Sew together pairs of red and green triangles. Press seam toward the green triangle.

3. Following the diagram, sew pairs of triangles together. Press seam toward the red/green triangle pair.

Make 8 units

4. Following the diagram, sew the blocks together into rows. Press seams as indicated.

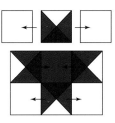

5. Sew the rows together. Press.

CORNER STAR BLOCK

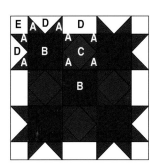

Make 2

1. Sew 1⅝" medium red squares onto the two corners of the white rectangles. Make 8 per block. Press as indicated.

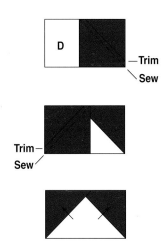

2. Sew 1⅝" medium red squares onto the four corners of the green squares. Make 4 per block. Press seam toward the red triangles.

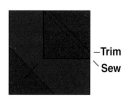

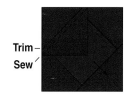

3. Arrange pieces as shown in the diagram. Sew together in horizontal rows. Press as indicated.

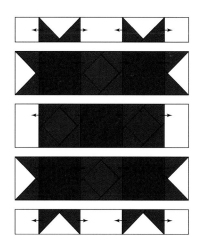

4. Sew rows together. Press.

TREE BLOCK

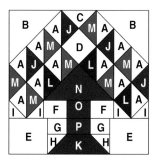

1. Following the block diagram, sew together pairs of A and J, A and L, and A and M triangles. Need 6 white/green pairs, 3 white/medium red pairs, and 3 white/dark red pairs. Press seams toward the red and green triangles.

2. Sew the G white rectangles to either side of the P dark green rectangle (middle portion of the tree trunk). Press seams toward the P rectangle.

3. Sew the H white squares to the dark red rectangle (K). Press seams toward the H triangles.

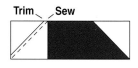

4. Sew the lower portion of the tree trunk (HKH unit) to the tree stand (GPG unit).

5. Sew the E white rectangles to both sides of the tree trunk and tree stand unit. Press seams toward E rectangles.

6. Sew the F white rectangles to both sides of the O dark green rectangle (upper portion of the tree trunk). Press seams toward the O rectangle.

7. Sew the small I white triangles to both ends of the upper tree trunk (FOF unit). Press seams toward the I triangles.

8. Sew the dark green N triangle to the upper portion of the tree trunk (IFOFI unit). Press seam toward the N triangle.

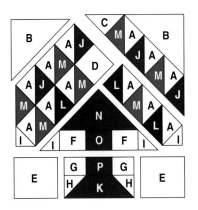

9. Following the diagram, lay out the pairs of triangles, single C, J, M, and I triangles, and D square. Sew together into diagonal rows as shown. Press seam toward red or green triangles.

10. In log cabin fashion, sew the pieced units as shown. Press.

11. Add the large white corner B triangles. Press seams toward the B triangles.

QUILT ASSEMBLY

1. Arrange blocks as shown in the Assembly Diagram on page 94.

2. Make three horizontal rows of blocks by sewing short sashing pieces between the blocks. Press seams toward the sashing.

3. Sew two horizontal rows of two square posts between three short sashing pieces. Press seams toward the square posts.

4. Sew the sashing rows between the rows of blocks. Press toward the sashing rows.

5. Sew a long sashing piece to the sides of the quilt. Press seams toward the side sashing.

6. Sew a square post to each end of the two remaining long sashing pieces, then sew them to the top and bottom of the quilt. Press seams toward the top and bottom sashing.

7. Sew the $1\frac{1}{2}$" x $31\frac{1}{2}$" white inner border strips to the top and bottom of the quilt. Press seams toward the inner border.

8. Sew the $1\frac{1}{2}$" x $32\frac{1}{2}$" white inner border strips to the sides of the quilt. Press seams toward the inner border.

9. Assemble the outer borders by sewing together the $2\frac{1}{2}$"-wide strips of medium green, dark red, dark green, and medium red into strip sets. Press. Cut into $3\frac{1}{2}$" sections and sew 4 groups of rectangles together so you end up with 4 strips of 16 rectangles each. Press.

10. Sew together red half-square triangles and white half-square triangles for the corner blocks. Make 4. Press seams toward the red triangle.

11. Sew two pieced borders to the sides of the quilt. Press seam toward the inner white border.

12. Sew corner blocks to each end of the two remaining pieced borders. Press seam toward the pieced border. Sew onto the top and bottom of the quilt. Press seams toward the inner white border.

QUILTING

The quiltmaker machine quilted in-the-ditch around each block and the major shapes within the block. She also machine quilted in-the-ditch on both sides of the white inner border so it "pops" out. Switching to hand quilting, the quilter used contrasting thread $1/4$" inside some shapes within the blocks and diagonally across others. The sashing was quilted with two parallel lines of contrasting thread; the corner posts were left unquilted. The pieced border was quilted with contrasting thread $1/4$" from each seam in each color section.

Quilt Assembly

Christmas Wreath of Roses Quilt

Machine appliquéd and quilted by Nancy Odom.

Small prints with an "almost solid" look work well with this pattern. You will need a bright red for
the flowers and border, white for the flower centers and background, and assorted shades of
green in a range from medium to medium dark. The quilter used the darkest green for the binding.

Use the appliqué technique of your choice to complete the blocks. Our quilter chose to fuse appliqué shapes onto the background squares and used a blanket stitch when she machine appliquéd the edges. You can choose to use the more traditional hand appliqué, using the needle-turn or freezer paper method; or machine stitch the appliqué pieces using a zigzag stitch.

Fabrics for the quilt shown were graciously donated by R.J.R. Fashion Fabrics from their Bare Essentials and Jinny Beyer Basic Realities collections. Thread was donated by Coats and Clark.

Finished Size: $38\frac{1}{2}$" square
Blocks Set: 3 x 3 blocks
Block Size: 12" finished

FABRIC REQUIREMENTS
White Background (and flower centers): $1\frac{1}{4}$ yards
Assorted Greens for Wreath Vine and Leaves: 1 yard for $\frac{1}{4}$"-wide finished bias strips. Leftover fabric can be used for leaves.
Bright Red for Border and Flowers: $\frac{1}{2}$ yard
Backing: $1\frac{1}{4}$ yards
Batting: 42" x 42"

Binding: $\frac{1}{2}$ yard of medium dark green
Bias bar: $\frac{1}{4}$" to create the center vine
Template plastic or fusible paper-backed adhesive

CUTTING
The template patterns for the flowers and leaves are on page 98.

White Background Squares: Cut three $13\frac{1}{2}$"-wide strips into nine squares. (Squares will be trimmed to $12\frac{1}{2}$" when appliqué is complete.)
White Flower Centers: Trace and cut 36.
Red Flowers: Trace and cut 36.
Green Leaves: Trace and cut 108 large and 72 small leaves.
Wreath Vine: Cut $\frac{7}{8}$"-wide bias strips to make a total of 162".

BORDERS
Before you cut the borders, follow the instructions in the General Guidelines (page 102), and check the final measurements of your quilt top. Adjust the border cutting lengths if necessary.

Sides: Cut two strips $2\frac{1}{2}$" x $36\frac{1}{2}$".

Top and Bottom: Cut two strips $2\frac{1}{2}$" x $40\frac{1}{2}$"

BLOCK ASSEMBLY
1. In preparation for appliqué, press each background square diagonally, vertically, and horizontally to find the center of the block and to create guideline folds. You can choose to lightly draw placement lines for the appliqué pieces on the base fabric. Be sure to draw the lines so they are about $\frac{1}{8}$" inside the actual outline of the shapes so the lines will be covered as you sew.

2. The outside edge of the vine forms a broken 8" diameter circle around the center of the block. Begin by creating the center vine sections for the wreath. The vine is made up of four individual pieces so it does not run behind the flowers. Cut the $\frac{7}{8}$"-wide bias strips into 36 pieces approximately $4\frac{1}{2}$" long. With wrong sides together, fold the bias strips in half lengthwise, and stitch about $\frac{1}{8}$" from the outside edge. Insert the bias bar, and press on both sides with the seam centered on the back.

3. Place the bias sections on the right side of the background fabric with the seam allowances facing down. Baste or lightly glue the vine sections in place, then appliqué both edges using your favorite method.

4. Arrange the four flowers covering the ends of the vine sections. Then baste, fuse, or glue in place. Appliqué each flower.

5. Position the flower centers according to the pattern, then baste, fuse, or glue in place. Appliqué each flower center.

6. Place the leaves according to the diagram, and baste, fuse, or glue in place. Appliqué the leaves.

QUILT TOP ASSEMBLY

1. Trim all blocks to 12½" square.

2. Sew the blocks into horizontal rows. Press the seams of alternate rows in opposite directions.

3. Sew the horizontal rows together. Press seams in one direction.

BORDERS

1. Follow the Assembly Diagram to add the borders. Pin and then sew the side border lengths, press toward the border. Add the top and bottom borders, press toward the border.

QUILTING

Our quilter used a poinsettia flower design in the centers of the wreaths and at the intersections of the blocks. She quilted in-the-ditch around the wreath and flowers, and added an echo line of stitching ¼" away from the first line of stitching. She also used a random meandering stitch for the rest of the quilt top, and a holly leaf design along the border. However, this pattern would look good with a grid pattern, or whatever design whimsy dictates.

Quilt Assembly

Half of the Wreath

8" outside diameter $\frac{1}{4}$" wide

Rotate to trace other half of circle. Adjust placement of leaves and flowers.

If hand appliquéing, add $\frac{3}{16}$" seam allowance. Trace the reversed leaves if using freezer paper or fusible adhesive.

Flower Center Trace 36

Flower Trace 36

Large Leaf Trace 108

Small Leaf Trace 72

Large Leaf, Reversed

Small Leaf, Reversed

Log Cabin Quilt ▶

CONCLUSION

I hope you have enjoyed my backroads tour of the special places in my life, and have found the time to make one or more of the quilt projects. It was such a thrill for me to see the quilts pictured in my paintings come alive through the efforts of the talented quiltmakers who made them specifically for this book. Until I find the time to add quiltmaking skills to my list of accomplishments, I'll continue to "make" quilts with my paintbrush. Have fun!

◀ *Sending Love*

The guidelines that follow are basic instructions. For more information please refer to the Bibliography, page 107.

Rotary cutting is used in the pieced projects.

Fabric: Use 100% cotton. We recommend prewashing all of your fabric, especially if you are planning to make a bed-size quilt that will require laundering. Wash darks and lights separately by hand or using the soak cycle on your machine, then machine dry on the permanent press setting. Some quilters feel that prewashing eliminates the chemicals used in the fabric printing process, making the fabrics softer and therefore easier to hand quilt.

Fabric requirements are based on a 42" width; many fabrics shrink when washed, and widths vary by manufacturer. In cutting instructions, strips are cut on the crosswise grain.

Supplies

* Sewing machine in good working order (We recommend starting any new project with a new needle.)
* Threads to match fabrics
* Scissors
* Iron and ironing board
* Pins
* Safety pins
* Template plastic
* Freezer paper (if desired for appliqué)
* Fusible adhesive (if you choose to fuse appliqué shapes to background fabric)
* Seam ripper

* Rulers: a 6" x 24" and a 15" square see-through acrylic ruler
* Rotary cutter and mat
* Marking tools
* Quilting thread
* Design Wall: can be a flannel-backed tablecloth or piece of batting tacked to a wall

Seam allowances: Use 1/4" for all pieced projects. It's a good idea to do a test seam before you begin sewing to check that your 1/4" is accurate.

Pressing: In general, press seams toward the darker fabric. Press lightly in an up-and-down motion. Avoid using a very hot iron or over-ironing, which can distort shapes and blocks.

Borders: Measurements are given for border strips to be cut on the crosswise grain. Diagonally piece the strips together to achieve the needed lengths.

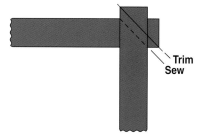

Overlap strips border strips right sides together, stitch diagonally from notch to notch.

Press seam open

Press seam open to distribute fabric layers.

In most cases the side borders are sewn on first. When you have finished the quilt top, measure it across the center vertically. This will be the length to cut for the side borders. Place pins at the centers and quarter points of all four sides of the quilt top, and do the same with each side border strip. Pin the side borders to the quilt top first, matching the center pins. Using a $1/4$" seam allowance, sew the borders to the quilt top and press. Measure horizontally across the center of the quilt top including the side borders. This will be the length to cut for the top and bottom borders. Repeat pinning, sewing, and pressing.

Backing: Use 100% cotton for the backing; plan on making the backing a minimum of 2" larger than the quilt top on all sides. Prewash the fabric, and trim the selvages before you piece. For small, square quilts less than 38" wide, you can buy $1\frac{1}{4}$ yards and trim to a square. To economize, you can piece the back from any leftover fabrics or blocks in your collection. Some ambitious quilters end up making two-sided quilts, or buy fabric and piece it according to the diagrams below. Backing yardages are based on these diagrams.

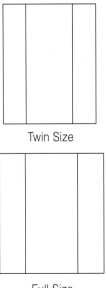

Twin Size

Full Size

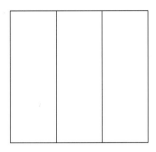

Queen or King Size

Batting: The type of batting to use is a personal decision; for a more traditional look consider using a very thin cotton batting, and then washing the quilt after you have finished quilting it. Some of the cotton battings can be bought by the yard; consult your local quilt shop. Cut batting approximately 2" larger on all sides than your quilt top.

Layering: Spread the backing wrong side up and tape the edges down with masking tape. (If you are working on carpet you can use T-pins to secure the backing to the carpet.) Center the batting on top, smooth out any folds. Place the quilt top right side up on top of the batting and backing, making sure it's centered.

Basting: If you plan to machine quilt, pin baste the quilt layers together with safety pins placed every 3"-4" apart. Begin basting in the center and move toward the edges first in vertical, then horizontal, rows.

If you plan to hand quilt, baste the layers together with thread using a long needle and light-colored thread. Knot one end of the thread. Using stitches approximately the length of the needle, begin in the center and move out toward the edges.

Quilting: Quilting, whether by hand or machine, enhances the pieced or appliqué design of the quilt. You may choose to quilt in-the-ditch, echo the pieced or appliqué motifs, or use patterns from quilting design books and stencils, or do your own free-motion quilting. Please refer to the Bibliography for more information about quilting.

Binding: Trim excess batting and backing from the quilt. If you want a $1/4$" finished binding, cut the strips 2" wide and piece together with a diagonal seam to make a continuous binding strip.

Fold to back and blind stitch

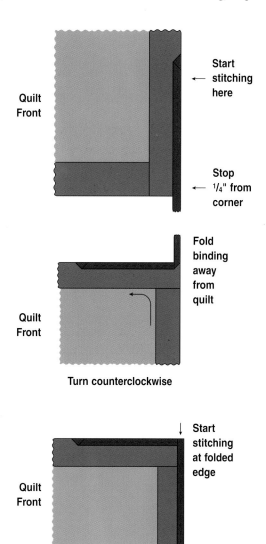

Press the seams open, then press the entire strip in half lengthwise with wrong sides together. With raw edges even, pin the binding to the edge of the quilt a few inches away from the corner, and leave the first few inches of the binding unattached. Start sewing, using a $1/4$" seam allowance.

Stop $1/4$" away from the first corner, backstitch one stitch, and pivot the quilt with the needle down into the quilt. Lift the needle and fold the binding at a right angle so it extends straight above the quilt. Then bring the binding strip down even with the edge of the quilt. Begin sewing at the folded edge. Repeat in the same manner at all corners. Finish off the binding by folding the beginning end in $1/4$" and overlapping it with the ending end, trimming any leftover binding. Fold the binding over the raw edge to the back of the quilt and blind stitch the binding to the back.

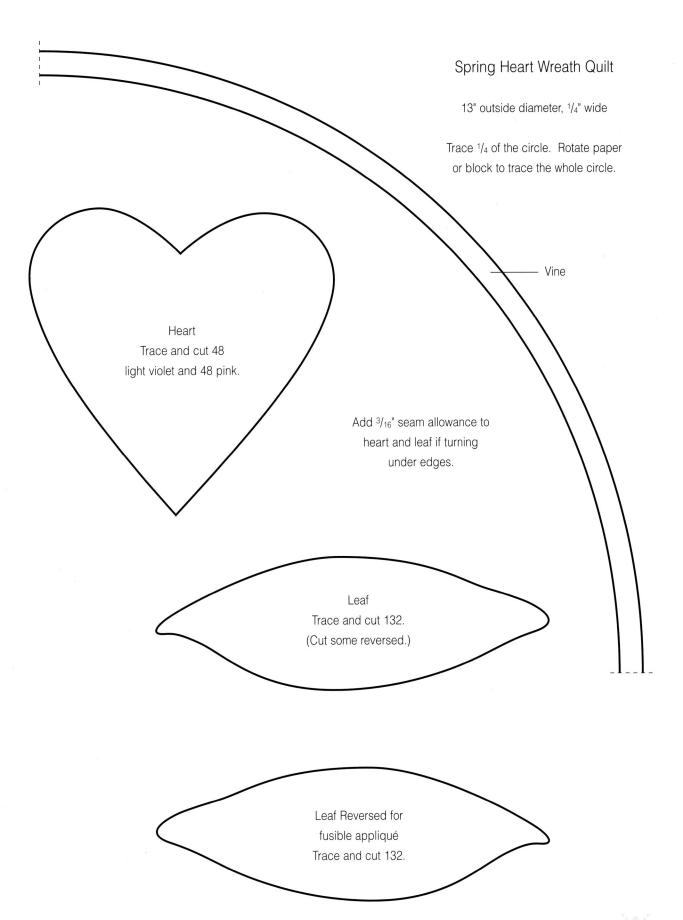

Spring Heart Wreath Quilt

13" outside diameter, $1/4$" wide

Trace $1/4$ of the circle. Rotate paper
or block to trace the whole circle.

Vine

Heart
Trace and cut 48
light violet and 48 pink.

Add $3/16$" seam allowance to
heart and leaf if turning
under edges.

Leaf
Trace and cut 132.
(Cut some reversed.)

Leaf Reversed for
fusible appliqué
Trace and cut 132.

105

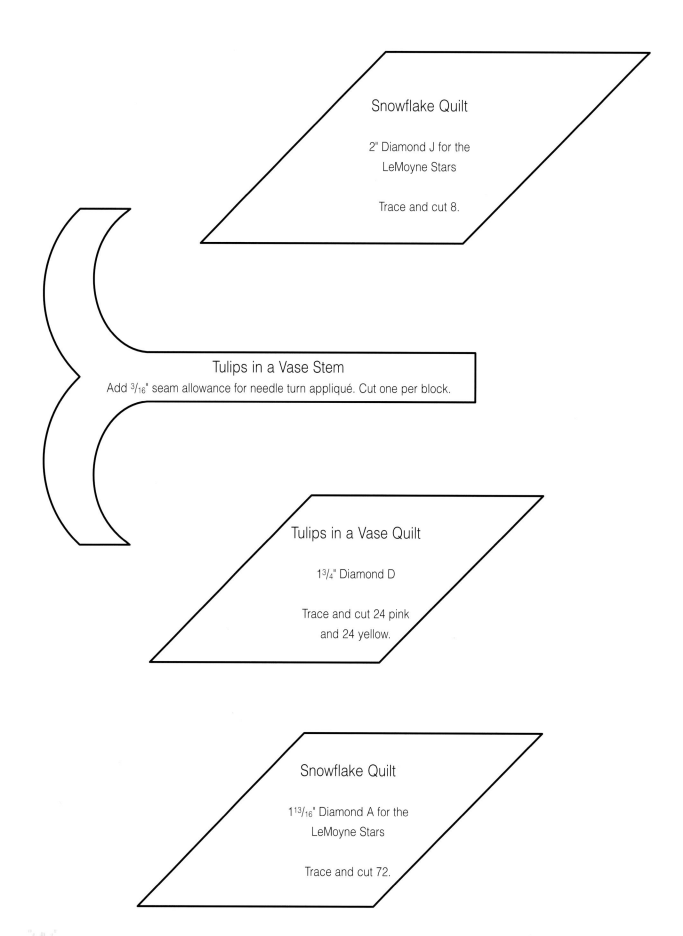

Snowflake Quilt

2" Diamond J for the
LeMoyne Stars

Trace and cut 8.

Tulips in a Vase Stem

Add 3/16" seam allowance for needle turn appliqué. Cut one per block.

Tulips in a Vase Quilt

1 3/4" Diamond D

Trace and cut 24 pink
and 24 yellow.

Snowflake Quilt

1 13/16" Diamond A for the
LeMoyne Stars

Trace and cut 72.

BIBLIOGRAPHY

Anderson, Alex.
Rotary Cutting with Alex Anderson: Tips•Techniques•Projects.
Lafayette, CA: C&T Publishing,1999.

Anderson, Alex.
Start Quilting with Alex Anderson: Six Projects for First-time Quilters.
Lafayette, CA: C&T Publishing,1997.

Cory, Pepper.
Mastering Quilt Marking: •Marking Tools & Techniques •Choosing Stencils •Matching Borders and Corners.
Lafayette, CA: C&T Publishing,1999.

Fons, Marianne and Liz Porter,
Quilter's Complete Guide.
Birmingham, AL: Oxmoor House, 1993.

Hargrave, Harriet and Sharyn Craig.
The Art of Classic Quiltmaking.
Lafayette, CA: C&T Publishing, 2000.

Hargrave, Harriet.
Heirloom Machine Quilting: A Comprehensive Guide to Hand Quilted Effects Using Your Sewing Machine, third edition.
Lafayette, CA: C&T Publishing,1995.

Hargrave, Harriet.
Mastering Machine Appliqué: The Satin Stitch, Mock Hand Appliqué and Other Techniques.
Lafayette, CA: C&T Publishing,1991.

Leone, Diana.
The New Sampler Quilt.
Lafayette, CA: C&T Publishing, 1993.

Sienkiewicz, Elly.
Appliqué 12 Easy Ways! Charming Quilts, Giftable Projects, & Timeless Techniques.
Lafayette, CA: C&T Publishing, 1991.

Diane Beginnes-Phalen was born and raised in Bethlehem, Pennsylvania. Her love of art and nature began in her early childhood years. She spent many hours every day sketching in the beautiful Pennsylvania coutnryside that surrounds her home. Although she currently resides in Banks, Oregon, Diane returns often to her native state to visit family and recall favorite childhood memories. She spends much of that time traveling the backroads of Pennsylvania, including the rustic Amish settlements of Lancaster County. It is here she finds the picturesque barns and covered bridges, country stores, and beautiful quilts she loves to paint.

Diane's goal is to convey to the viewers and collectors of her paintings the smell of flowers, the feeling of a warm summer day or cooling breeze, the mood of an autumn sky or winter sunset, and the peace and contentment of nature and her Pennsylvania heriteage. Diane is best-known for her continuing *Americana Quilt Series*, of which prints, posters, notecards, and gift items are distributed worldwide.

▼ Diane, Bogie, Gato, Socks, and Oz

Appliqué 12 Easy Ways!: Charming Quilts, Giftable Projects & Timeless Techniques, Elly Sienkiewicz

Art & Inspirations: Ruth B. McDowell, Ruth B. McDowell

The Art of Classic Quiltmaking, Harriet Hargrave and Sharyn Craig

Civil War Women: Their Quilts, Their Roles, and Activities for Re-Enactors, Barbara Brackman

Color From the Heart: Seven Great Ways to Make Quilts with Colors You Love, Gai Perry

Color Play: Easy Steps for Imaginative Color in Quilts, Joen Wolfrom

Curves in Motion: Quilt Designs & Techniques, Judy B. Dales

Deidre Scherer: Work in Fabric & Thread, Deidre Scherer

Fabric Shopping with Alex Anderson, Seven Projects to Help You: Make Successful Choices, Build Your Confidence, Add to Your Fabric Stash, Alex Anderson

Fancy Appliqué: 12 Lessons to Enhance Your Skills, Elly Sienkiewicz

Fantastic Fabric Folding: Innovative Quilting Projects, Rebecca Wat

Freddy's House: Brilliant Color in Quilts, Freddy Moran

Free Stuff for Collectors on the Internet, Judy Heim and Gloria Hansen

Free Stuff for Crafty Kids on the Internet, Judy Heim and Gloria Hansen

Free Stuff for Quilters on the Internet, 2nd Ed. Judy Heim and Gloria Hansen

Free Stuff for Sewing Fanatics on the Internet, Judy Heim and Gloria Hansen

Free Stuff for Stitchers on the Internet, Judy Heim and Gloria Hansen

From Fiber to Fabric: The Essential Guide to Quiltmaking Textiles, Harriet Hargrave

Hand Quilting with Alex Anderson: Six Projects for Hand Quilters, Alex Anderson

Heirloom Machine Quilting, Third Edition, Harriet Hargrave

Impressionist Palette, Gai Perry

Kaleidoscopes & Quilts, Paula Nadelstern

Make Any Block Any Size, Joen Wolfrom

Mastering Machine Appliqué, Harriet Hargrave

Mastering Quilt Marking: Marking Tools & Techniques, Choosing Stencils, Matching Borders & Corners, Pepper Cory

Patchwork Persuasion: Fascinating Quilts from Traditional Designs, Joen Wolfrom

Pieced Flowers, Ruth B. McDowell

Piecing: Expanding the Basics, Ruth B. McDowell

The Quilted Garden: Design and Make Nature-Inspired Quilts, Jane Sassaman

Quilting with the Muppets, The Jim Henson Company in Association with Children's Television Workshop

Quilts from Europe, Projects and Inspiration, Gül Laporte

Quilts from the Civil War: Nine Projects, Historical Notes, Diary Entries, Barbara Brackman

Shadow Quilts: Easy-to-Design Multiple Image Quilts, Patricia Magaret and Donna Slusser

Smashing Sets: Exciting Ways to Arrange Quilt Blocks, Margaret Miller

Special Delivery Quilts, Patrick Lose

Start Quilting with Alex Anderson: Six Projects for First-Time Quilters, Alex Anderson

Through the Garden Gate: Quilters and Their Gardens, Jean and Valori Wells

Travels with Peaky and Spike: Doreen Speckmann's Quilting Adventures, Doreen Speckmann

The Visual Dance: Creating Spectacular Quilts, Joen Wolfrom

Wild Birds: Designs for Appliqué & Quilting, Carol Armstrong

Wildflowers: Designs for Appliqué & Quilting, Carol Armstrong

Willowood: Further Adventures in Buttonhole Stitch Appliqué, Jean Wells

Women of Taste: A Collaboration Celebrating Quilt Artists and Chefs, Girls, Inc.

Yvonne Porcella: Art & Inspirations, Yvonne Porcella

For more information write for a free catalog:
C&T Publishing, Inc.
P.O. Box 1456, Lafayette, CA 94549
(800) 284-1114
http://www.ctpub.com
e-mail: ctinfo@ctpub.com

For quilting supplies:
Cotton Patch Mail Order
3405 Hall Lane, Dept. CTB, Lafayette, CA 94549
e-mail: quiltusa@yahoo.com
web: www.quiltusa.com
(800) 835-4418
(925) 283-7883